# *Clay v. United States* and How Muhammad Ali Fought the Draft

## Debating Supreme Court Decisions

*Tom Streissguth*

**Enslow Publishers, Inc.**

| | |
|---|---|
| 40 Industrial Road | PO Box 38 |
| Box 398 | Aldershot |
| Berkeley Heights, NJ 07922 | Hants GU12 6BP |
| USA | UK |

http://www.enslow.com

Copyright © 2006 by Tom Streissguth

**Library of Congress Cataloging-in-Publication Data**

Streissguth, Thomas, 1958–
     Clay v. United States and how Muhammad Ali fought the draft : debating Supreme
Court decisions / Tom Streissguth.
        p. cm. — (Debating Supreme Court decisions)
     Includes bibliographical references and index.
     ISBN 0-7660-2393-1
     1.  Ali, Muhammad, 1942—Trials, litigation, etc.—Juvenile literature. 2. Trials
(Political crimes and offenses)—United States—History—20th century—Juvenile
literature. 3. Conscientious objectors—Legal status, laws, etc.—United States—
History—20th century—Juvenile literature. 4. Draft—Law and legislation—United
States—History—20th century—Juvenile literature.  I. Title: Clay versus United States
and how Muhammad Ali fought the draft. II. Title. III. Series.
KF224.A47S77 2005
343.73'0126'0269—dc22

                                                2005019439


Printed in the United States of America

10 9 8 7 6 5 4 3 2 1

**To Our Readers:** We have done our best to make sure that all Internet Addresses in this
book were active and appropriate when we went to press. However, the author and
publisher have no control over and assume no liability for the material available on those
Internet sites or on other Web sites they may link to. Any comments or suggestions can be
sent by e-mail to comments@enslow.com or to the address on the back cover.

**Illustration Credits:** All photos are from AP/Wide World, except as follows:
Library of Congress, p. 22; Harris and Ewing, Collection of the Supreme Court of
the United States, p. 35.

**Cover Illustration:** Background: Artville; photograph: AP/Wide World.

# Contents

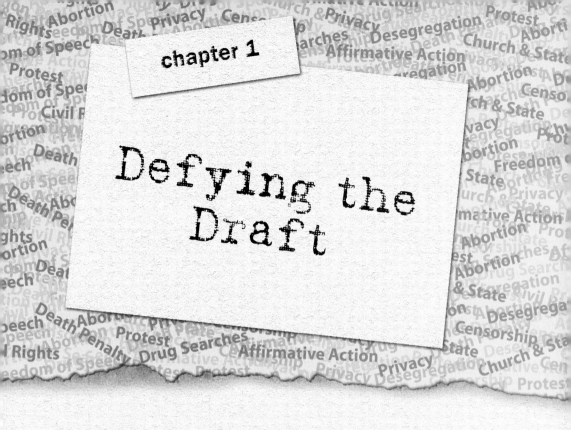

# chapter 1

# Defying the Draft

At 8:00 A.M. on April 28, 1967, Muhammad Ali arrived at the United States Armed Forces Examining and Entrance Station on San Jacinto Street in Houston, Texas. Making his way through a crowd of reporters and onlookers, Ali looked calm and determined. But his appearance did not match the strong emotions, both fearful and defiant, churning within. In his boxing career, he had fought and defeated many powerful opponents. Although he was famous for his self-confidence, he also knew he was now facing a very tough battle. The outcome of this fight would decide the direction of his life for many years to come.

He had arrived a half hour early to avoid a crowd. But his plan had failed. On San Jacinto Street, all eyes were on him; some people were shouting encouragement, while others were ridiculing him. The entire country was watching and waiting because this event involved much more than the drafting of a young man for military service. That day, San Jacinto Street became the center of the bitter national debate over the war in Vietnam.

Ali and the other inductees filed into the building. Men in crisp military uniforms herded them into a large hall and handed them several forms to fill out. Doctors put each one through a medical examination, then directed them to a cafeteria for lunch: two sandwiches, an apple, and cake. At 1:00 P.M., the lunch hour ended, and escorts brought the men to their next assembly in the "ceremony room." They formed several straight lines before the induction officer, who announced:

> You are about to be inducted into the Armed Forces of the United States, in the Army, the Navy, the Air Force, or the Marine Corps, as indicated by the service announced following your name when called. You will take one step forward as your name and service are called, and such step will constitute your induction into the Armed Forces indicated.[1]

One by one, names were called, followed by the name of a service branch—usually "Army." The room fell completely silent. Only the stern and clipped voice of the induction officer could be heard. The ceremony proceeded quickly, with each man stepping quietly forward, until the name of "Cassius Marcellus Clay" was called.

This was Muhammad Ali's former name, and he was accustomed to having people use it. But the name was a symbol of his past—before his conversion to Islam—and he usually reacted to it by simply ignoring it. This time, his reaction was just the same. He did nothing.

Lieutenant Clarence Hartman walked up to Ali and asked him to step aside. Hartman brought him to a small private room and explained the possible consequences of refusing induction: five years in jail and a ten thousand dollar fine. He brought Ali back to the hall, where the name of Cassius Clay was called again, and where Muhammad Ali again refused to step forward. Ali was then asked to write down the reasons for his refusal. He wrote: "I refuse to be inducted into the armed forces of the United States because I claim to be exempt as a minister of the religion of Islam."[2]

That day, while a group of new soldiers traveled from Houston to basic training at Fort Polk, Louisiana, one man stayed behind to begin a long battle in the press, in the courts, and within himself. The commanding officer of the Houston induction center announced to the press:

> Ladies and gentlemen; Cassius Clay has just refused to be inducted into the United States Armed Forces. Notification of his refusal is being made to the United States Attorney, the State Director of the Selective Service System, and the

local Selective Service Board for whatever action is deemed appropriate.[3]

Muhammad Ali had claimed to be a conscientious objector: someone whose religious and/or philosophical beliefs prevented him from joining the military or fighting a war. Following the example of thousands, going back to the American Revolution, he had refused to submit to a military draft. The military sent him home, and soon the United States would indict him for refusing induction into the Army. His case would continue for four years.

While the courts heard his case, Muhammad Ali managed to keep his freedom. But the law and the higher authorities of the boxing world abruptly stopped his career just as he was reaching his prime. Some saw him as a sincere conscientious objector, while others—the majority—saw him as a cowardly draft dodger. His success in the boxing ring and his worldwide fame made him the focus of opposition to the draft and the war. If he was truly sincere in his beliefs, the law excused him. If he was not, then he was liable to spend five years in jail. The verdict would soon come down, and it then would be appealed. In this particular battle, neither the federal government nor Muhammad Ali would throw in the towel. There was only one place for the final decision in *Clay* v. *United States*: the Supreme Court.

*Champion boxer Muhammad Ali is escorted from the Armed Forces Examining and Entrance Station in Houston, Texas, after refusing to be inducted into the armed forces.*

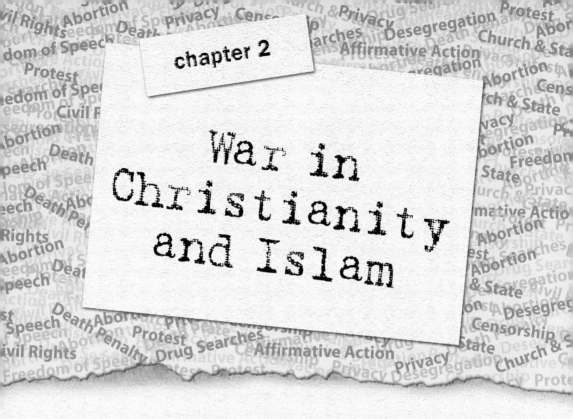

# chapter 2

# War in Christianity and Islam

Since ancient times, people of all faiths and nationalities have argued about war. The first Christians, whose religion was banned and who lived under the threat of execution in the Roman Empire, refused to fight for the empire. Their holy books, later collected into the New Testament, preached submission to their enemies and nonviolence. For example, in the Gospel of Luke, Chapter 6, verses 27–29, this philosophy is explained by Jesus:

> But if you are willing to listen, I say, love your enemies. Do good to those who hate you. Pray for the happiness of those who curse you. Pray for those who hurt you. If someone slaps you on one cheek, turn the other cheek. If someone demands your coat, offer your shirt also.

In the fourth century, the Roman emperor Constantine adopted Christianity as the official state religion. Soon afterward, the Christian bishop and philosopher St. Augustine expounded a doctrine of "just war." Under certain conditions, joining the army and fighting one's enemies became acceptable. The doctrine allows war if done in self-defense, if legally declared by the highest authorities, and if used as a last resort. In addition, a "just war" should be fought proportionately—meaning one should not deliberately increase the death and destruction it causes. Finally, fighting must have as its final goal a just and lasting peace.

## The Jihad of Islam

Two centuries after St. Augustine, an Arab trader and visionary named Muhammad founded the religion of Islam. This new faith spread rapidly among the people of Arabia. Islamic armies conquered the Middle East, North Africa, Spain, and Persia. Nonbelievers were killed in battle or imprisoned, while many others converted to the faith. In some Islamic societies, "infidels" (nonbelievers), including Christians and Jews, were accepted as outsiders. They could practice their faith but were subject to Islamic laws and authority.

The holy book of Islam, the Koran, urges believers to fight for the faith. Jihad, or "holy war," was the Islamic version of the Christian "just war." Its purpose was not only self-defense, or defense of the faith. Muslim religious leaders could summon followers to holy war to convert nonbelievers. Islamic leaders declared jihad through edicts (spoken or written pronouncements). An edition of the Koran from the eighteenth century translates one such command to jihad as follows:

> God . . . commandeth you to fight his battles, that he may prove the one of you by the other. And as to those who fight in defence of God's true religion, God will not suffer their works to perish; he will guide them, and will dispose their heart aright; and he will lead them into paradise, of which he hath told them. O true believers, if ye assist God, by fighting for his religion, he will assist you against your enemies; and will set your feet fast. . . .[1]

Islam's rapid spread made it Christianity's chief rival during the Middle Ages. Christian and Islamic armies clashed in Spain, France, and the Balkan Peninsula. Christian kings sent armies to capture the holy city of Jerusalem from its Islamic rulers. These Crusades lasted two centuries, until the fall of the last Crusader stronghold in 1291. The Crusades left lasting bitterness between Christians and Muslims, particularly in the Middle East.

In the centuries after the Crusades, Islam spread further across Asia. A Muslim empire was established in northern India, and Muslim traders brought the faith to Malaysia and Indonesia. In 1453, the Muslim Turks of the Ottoman Empire captured Constantinople (modern Istanbul), an outpost of Christianity at the southeastern limit of Europe. Ottoman conquests following this event brought Islam to Greece, Bosnia, and other corners of the Balkan Peninsula.

Battles were also being fought among European Christians. In the late Middle Ages, Protestant sects arose in central Europe. These sects opposed the power and corruption of the dominant Roman Catholic Church. Several Protestant sects took up pacifism and the antiwar preachings of Jesus to "love thine enemy" and "turn the other cheek." Some of these sects (also called "peace churches") were the Anabaptists, Mennonites, Brethren, and the Society of Friends, or Quakers. Members of these sects often suffered discrimination, violence, and harassment at the hands of the authorities and of their fellow Christians. (Later peace churches that refused to take part in war in any form included the nineteenth-century Seventh-Day Adventists and the Jehovah's Witnesses, which was founded in the twentieth century.)

## Pacifism in the New World

The settlement of North America by European colonists brought the peace churches across the Atlantic Ocean. The Quakers and others were seeking the freedom to practice their beliefs in peace. The refusal of the Quakers to serve earthly rulers, such as the king of England, had marked them for persecution by the English Puritans. Once in North America, the Quakers would not join the colonial militias fighting the French and Indian War of the 1760s, when Britain fought for control of the frontiers against the French and their American Indian allies.

In the 1770s, the colonists rebelled against direct rule by England. Their representatives in the Continental Congress recognized "conscientious objectors" who belonged to the pacifist sects of Christianity. To fight for independence, the Continental Congress relied on volunteer soldiers and money contributed by the individual colonies.

On July 18, 1775, three months after the first shots of the war were fired, a resolution of Congress called on all men between the ages of sixteen and fifty to join their colony's militias. Each militia company would be made up of one captain, two lieutenants, one ensign, four sergeants, four corporals, one clerk, one drummer, one fifer, and sixty-eight privates. One fourth of the militia companies were to be selected as "minutemen." The minutemen had to be ready on short notice for defense against a British invasion or attack. Every four months, the minutemen had the opportunity to resign from this service, to be replaced by a draft from the "regular" volunteers. This draft of regulars for minuteman service was the first conscription of any kind in North America.

The resolution of the Continental Congress also recognized conscientious objectors:

> As there are some people, who, from religious principles, cannot bear arms in any case, this Congress intend no violence to their consciences, but earnestly recommend it to them, to contribute liberally in this time of universal calamity, to the relief of their distressed brethren in the several colonies, and to do all other services to their oppressed Country, which they can consistently with their religious principles.[2]

The Congress did not rule the individual colonies, however. The resolution served as guidance to colonial legislatures. Each of the colonies had its own law about conscientious objectors. They usually required conscientious objectors to pay a fine or hire a substitute to fight in their place. After independence was achieved, the state constitutions of Delaware, Pennsylvania, New York, and New Hampshire officially recognized conscientious objection on the basis of religious beliefs in their state constitutions.

After independence, the United States established a federal government in Washington, D.C. The Constitution guided the founders of the country in setting up the new federal system: Congress, the presidency, the courts, and federal law. The first ten amendments to the Constitution were known as the Bill of Rights. The Bill of Rights set down the legal rights of citizens. The First Amendment established freedom of speech and religion. The First Amendment—and later the Fourteenth—would become very important for the courts and the law.

The U.S. Constitution authorized the federal (national) legislature to organize, arm, and discipline the state militias. The federal government also had the power to summon the militias in case of a national emergency. The states had the authority to train these militias and appoint officers to lead them. Many members of Congress and colonial leaders opposed standing (permanent) armies, which had done so much to impose the tyranny of the English king on North America. Instead, each citizen would be obligated to serve in a local militia, if called upon.

The Constitution never resolved the issue of a permanent standing army or mentioned the use of a military draft. Volunteer armies fought in the War of 1812 and in the Mexican War of 1848–1849. But the Mexican War inspired some people to object publicly. Believing the war was meant to expand slavery to the western frontier, the writer Henry David Thoreau refused to pay taxes to protest. He went to jail for his stand.

# Conscription in the Civil War

In Thoreau's time, the issue of slavery divided the nation. In Southern states, the institution was legal, while in the North, it had been banned since the late eighteenth century. The importation of slaves anywhere into the country was made illegal in 1808. When a candidate opposed to the expansion of slavery, Abraham Lincoln, won the presidential election of 1860, the Southern states began to secede from the union. In early 1861, the seceding states formed a Confederate States of America. In April, Confederate and Union armies fired the first shots of the Civil War.

The Civil War demanded a total industrial and military effort on both sides. The federal and Confederate governments realized that all-volunteer armies would not be strong enough to win. To gather soldiers to fight, the U.S. Congress passed the Federal Militia Act in 1862. This law called on the Union states to begin conscription to fill the ranks of their militias. The militias would fight alongside the "regulars"—volunteer members of the United States Army. Militia units would take orders from Army generals. General Order Number 99, issued by the adjutant general, allowed the states to exempt conscientious objectors (COs). The military only recognized members of peace churches as sincere conscientious objectors.

In October 1862, the Confederacy also passed a

conscription law. This law also exempted members of the peace churches. It also allowed those who could hire a substitute to fight in their place to do so. A man could also pay a five hundred dollar "commutation fee" instead of serving. At the time of the Civil War, five hundred dollars was a lot of money to a worker, in the North as well as the South. Only the rich could afford to pay the commutation fee.

In 1863, Congress passed the Federal Conscription Act, setting down rules for the substitution system in the Union. Those who could pay a commutation fee of three hundred dollars—equal to a year's salary for many—or get a substitute could escape conscription. The Draft Act of February 1864 also exempted members of religious denominations opposed to the bearing of arms. The law did not provide for noncombat service for COs.

The new laws inspired a violent reaction in many Northern cities. Workers and immigrants who had no personal grudge against slavery or interest in saving the Union resisted military service. Many refused to report to induction offices and violently protested the commutation fee. Some rampaged through Northern cities, burning and looting them. Street riots broke out in several of the largest cities. The most deadly riot occurred in New York, where massive crowds of draft opponents battled armies of police. Rioters lynched free African Americans by the dozens.

Those who claimed to be conscientious objectors but did not belong to peace churches were expected to put on a uniform. Their claim of conscientious objector status followed them into the ranks, where they were often treated brutally as slackers and would-be deserters by their officers.

In both North and South, drafted COs were sometimes mistreated in attempts to make them fight. According to one historical account, "Some objectors were strung up by their thumbs, tied down in a crouch, pricked with bayonets, threatened with execution, or prodded into battle with muskets tied to their backs."[3]

The draft laws expired at the end of the Civil War. The military returned to a much smaller, all-volunteer force. This force was employed to subdue Indians resisting white settlement in the western United States and to fight the Spanish-American War of 1898. In Europe, meanwhile, war clouds gathered again in the early twentieth century. Two grand alliances formed, with France and Germany preparing to fight across their mutual frontier. War broke out in the summer of 1914, when Germany invaded Belgium and France. The United States stayed out of the conflict until 1917. The draft returned—as did the debate on conscientious objectors.

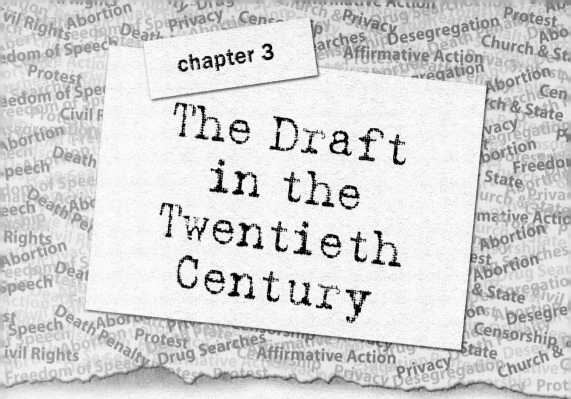

# chapter 3

# The Draft in the Twentieth Century

Many Americans saw World War I as a European problem. "Isolationists" spoke out against any American involvement. Recent immigrants from Germany were against fighting on the side of the Allies: France, Great Britain, and Russia. Socialists opposed to the imperial government of Russia opposed fighting as an ally of the Russian tsar (emperor). Many people saw the war as a waste of blood and money in the service of corrupt European governments.

Nevertheless, others demanded that the United States enter the war on the side of the Allies and oppose Germany's assault on France. In 1917, the U.S. Congress declared war on Germany. The Draft Act of that year authorized the induction of

3 million men by lottery. To carry out the lottery, the government set up the Selective Service. This was a new civilian agency responsible for inducting men for military service. The system operated through a network of local draft boards. Local and state governments appointed officials to the draft boards. When additional men were needed by the military, the government assigned a quota for each branch of service to the boards. The draft boards came up with lists of inductees, sent out notices, and gathered the draftees for transportation to military camps. The boards also reported those who did not comply with the induction process to the federal government for prosecution.

By the 1917 act, members of recognized peace churches were again exempted from conscription:

> nothing in this Act shall be construed to require or compel any person to serve in any of the forces herein provided for who is found to be a member of any well-recognized religious sect or organization at present organized and existing and whose existing creed or principles forbid its members to participate in war in any form . . . but no person so exempted shall be exempted from service in any capacity that the President shall declare to be noncombatant.[1]

During World War I, draftees could not hire substitutes or pay a fine to escape service. Congress saw these practices as unjustly favoring the wealthy. Congress also rejected conscientious

*The United States instituted its first military draft during World War I, and opposition was widespread. Shown here are men under armed guard because they were on the streets without their draft registration cards.*

objector status for those who did not belong to peace churches. The law did not admit objectors who "selectively" opposed the United States's entry into the war. By this doctrine, a draftee could not pick his fights—either he joined the military in any and all wars declared by the federal government or he was charged with draft evasion.

During World War I, sixty-five thousand draftees claimed to be conscientious objectors. Of these, twenty-one thousand had their claims rejected and were eventually inducted into the army. Many of these unwilling soldiers were subject to brutal treatment by officers and by fellow enlisted men. Others served with distinction. One conscientious objector, Alvin York, was a young farmer from Tennessee. A member of the Church of Christ in Christian Union, York took seriously the church's ban on fighting, either on his own or for the military. When he received his draft notice in 1917, he simply wrote "I don't want to fight" and returned it.

York eventually complied with the draft, however, and reported for training to Camp Gordon, Georgia. Under the persuasion of General George Edward Buxton, his battalion commander, York abandoned his objection to the conflict, sailed to France, and fought with great courage. He became the war's most celebrated American hero.

## Conscientious Objectors and World War II

In the United States, the debate over conscientious objectors continued in the courts, in government, and in academic institutions. Some of the most powerful words of this debate appeared in "The Conscientious Objector," an article written in 1919 by Harlan Fiske Stone, dean of Columbia Law School and later Chief Justice of the Supreme Court:

> Their evident sincerity and willingness to suffer to the end rather than to yield up their cherished illusion make impossible the wholesale

> condemnation of the conscientious objector as a coward and a slacker. . . . both morals and sound policy require that the state should not violate the conscience of the individual. All our history gives confirmation to the view that liberty of conscience has a moral and social value which makes it worthy of preservation at the hands of the state.[2]

Stone and others believed that government should excuse sincere conscientious objectors from military service. Others disagreed, claiming that the law unfairly favored some citizens on the basis of their religious belief. In wartime, this side argued, the nation needed some of its citizens to fight. Every man able to fight should be subject to the draft. Nearly all agreed that the law should require COs to perform noncombat service.

The divide over foreign wars also continued after World War I. Some wanted the United States to fight only in self-defense. The United States, by this view, should not get involved in the conflicts of other nations. Others saw the United States emerging as a world power. Such a power had to protect its interests all over the globe. If necessary, the United States should also fight for its allies, wherever they may be.

In the meantime, the harsh terms imposed on Germany after its defeat in World War I created an economic depression. The Germans felt a rising tide of resentment. An Austrian-born veteran named Adolf Hitler used this popular anger to bring his Nazi party to victory in the parliamentary elections of 1932. The German president, Paul von Hindenburg, then appointed Hitler chancellor, or chief minister, of Germany in January 1933. In violation of the World War I treaties, Hitler rapidly built up the German military and imposed a universal draft on German citizens.

In 1939, the debate over conscientious objectors became more urgent with the outbreak of World War II. Germany, under Hitler's leadership, attacked Poland. France and Great Britain declared war on Germany. The United States stayed out of the war for the time being. But President Franklin Roosevelt and members of Congress saw American involvement coming. To prepare, in 1940 Congress passed the Selective Training and Service Act, a law that prepared the country for another military draft.

This law was the first peacetime draft in U.S. history. It authorized the federal government to induct 1.2 million men for twelve months of military training. According to the law, the category of conscientious objector now included anyone "who, by reason of religious training and belief, is conscientiously opposed to participation in war in any form."[3]

After Germany's ally, Japan, attacked Pearl Harbor, Hawaii, on December 7, 1941, the United States declared war on the Axis powers—Japan,

Germany, and Italy. The government drafted 10 million men during World War II. Five million men and women volunteered for service. Fifty thousand draftees were classified as conscientious objectors. Nine out of ten of these COs claimed their status on the basis of membership in peace churches.

Most conscientious objectors served in the medical corps, taking care of sick and wounded men. However, twelve thousand COs refused to take part in any military activity whatsoever. One of these, Herman Will, stated his objection to an interviewer:

> I wouldn't be dissuaded by somebody trying to tell me that your point of view isn't practical—you know, it's not going to work, you can't resist Nazism by pacifist methods, or something like that. I just believe, as a religious person, I should not take human life, and it's that simple.[4]

Will and the others were assigned instead to domestic nonmilitary projects, such as construction and forestation. Many of them lived in Civilian Public Service (CPS) camps. The traditional peace churches operated these camps under the guidance of the Selective Service. The CPS camps were closed down after the war's end in 1945.

A small minority of about five thousand men did not register for the draft or were refused conscientious objector status. The federal government indicted them for breaking the law; the courts found them guilty and sentenced them to jail. Of these, about two hundred were Black Muslims. This sect, made up mostly of young African-American men, observed the rites of Islam. They objected to military service on the grounds that World War II was not a holy war as defined in the Koran.

## The Postwar Draft

The 1940 draft law was allowed to expire in 1947. World War II had been over for two years, and the military did not need draftees to serve. But the world was not at peace. The United States and the Soviet Union had emerged as rival superpowers. The superpowers had very different economic and political systems. They also had powerful militaries and nuclear weapons. In the opinion of many, Communism threatened a spread of totalitarian government around the world.

Within the United States, military planners prepared for a possible war with the Soviet Union or with its ally, Communist China. The United States also sought to prevent Soviet Communism from spreading to smaller countries in Latin America, Africa, and Asia. This "Cold War" rivalry over political and military allies threatened a third world war between the superpowers. The Selective Service was at the ready. If the military needed young men to fight, the draft would return.

With the Cold War between the United States

and the Soviet Union in mind, Congress quickly replaced the 1940 draft law with the Selective Service Act of 1948. The new law defined a conscientious objector's "religious training and belief" to mean ". . . an individual's belief in a relation to a Supreme Being involving duties superior to those arising from any human relation, [but does] not include essentially political, sociological, or philosophical views or a merely personal moral code."[5]

The law required men to register with their local draft board on their eighteenth birthday or immediately afterward. For each draftee, the local draft boards decided on one of eighteen draft classifications, including 1-A (fit for active duty), 1-S (student), 2-C (farmer), 4-D (minister), and 4-F (not qualified for military service). The draft classifications allowed "deferments" (delays). One could delay being drafted if one was a student, farmer, minister, or belonged to one of several other categories. To call up men for service, lotteries were held every year. Each day of the year was randomly assigned a different number. The lower the number that fell on one's birthday, the better the chances of being called up.

When called up for duty, a draftee had a six-year obligation to the military. After basic training, he could volunteer for the reserves, which meant six months of active duty and five and a half years of weekend drills. Reservists also had to report to a two-week camp in summer. The military had the option of extending tours of active duty, if necessary, during a declared war. It also could call up reserves in case of urgently needed troops.

In 1951, while American troops were fighting in the Korean War, the law was renamed the Universal Military Training and Service Act. During this war, in which the United States fought against Communist troops on the Korean peninsula, 1.5 million men were drafted. Of these, about 1½ percent were granted conscientious objector status.

Those claiming to be conscientious objectors had to fill out a questionnaire and explain the specific religious beliefs that prohibited their going to war. They also had to give evidence of these beliefs. Evidence meant public expression of their antiwar views. The conscientious objector had to show that he had spoken out or written against war—not just the Korean War, but all war. Local draft boards then evaluated the evidence. The board also interviewed the conscientious objector, and if necessary called witnesses to testify. If the board denied the CO claim, the objector could report for duty, or take his case to an appeal board.

## Appealing the Draft

The job of appeal boards was to make the final decision on conscientious objector status. First, the case was sent to the Department of Justice (DOJ). The DOJ is the country's federal prosecutor. It investigates suspects who break federal laws, such as the draft law. Its lawyers take criminals to court and bring evidence and testimony against them. A branch of the DOJ, the Federal Bureau of Investigation (FBI), assists the DOJ in this job.

If a conscientious objector appealed, the FBI conducted an investigation. FBI agents interviewed people and collected evidence. The FBI could also secretly conduct searches and record conversations. After the FBI finished its investigation, the DOJ then held a hearing. The conscientious objector could bring witnesses and evidence to the hearing. The hearing officer then made a report on the case and a recommendation either to uphold or to deny CO status. This report was sent back to the local appeal board, which then made the final decision. If conscientious objector status was denied, and the claimant still refused to appear or to step forward at the induction ceremony, the federal government could begin a criminal prosecution.

In some cases, conscientious objectors declared themselves after entering the military. At present, as in the past, those serving in the military are subject to military law. Each branch of service has its own code dealing with conscientious objectors.

Military courts, not federal civilian courts, decide these cases. The penalties can be harsh, and those found guilty have no right of appeal. A conscientious objector who refuses to fight while in the armed forces can go to prison. He or she can be charged with refusing to obey orders or desertion. If found guilty, he or she may lose rank and pay or be dishonorably discharged from the service.

## CO Status: The Pros and Cons

Those opposed to the conscientious objector law feel that everyone should share equally in the burden of defending the country. The CO law creates an unfair legal loophole, in this view. It allows those too fearful or lazy to escape military service, simply by writing a cleverly worded explanation or making a good presentation before a draft board. Worse, the original reason for legal CO status—that it was the free exercise of religious belief—no longer holds true. In a series of cases in the 1960s, the Supreme Court decided that conscientious objectors do not need to base their actions on religious belief. According to these decisions, they do not even have to belong to an established church. In the meantime, those without good legal advice, or those who do not understand the law, must accept their burden and risk their lives. This unfairly places the risks of military service on the poor, less educated, and less wealthy members of society.

Those supporting conscientious objection make the case that someone opposed to war, and to the government's decision to go to war, should not have to fight. They point out that conscription of a sincere CO will create more problems for the military than it will solve. A conscientious objector will resist military training, consider disobeying orders or deserting, and fight ineffectively. He or she will also spread antiwar views to others—volunteers and conscripts. The end result will be lower morale on the part of many, instead of the loss of service of a single individual. In any case, American citizens have the right to express their views and to resist government decisions they oppose. Such a right is a cornerstone of the U.S. Constitution and its First Amendment, which guarantees freedom of speech.

The Cold War turned hot in Vietnam in the 1960s. This time, the draft would become the center of the national debate over war. It would also claim a young professional boxer who was prepared to fight it all the way to the Supreme Court.

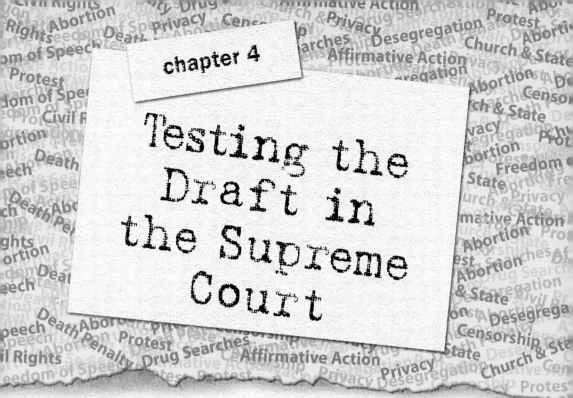

# chapter 4

# Testing the Draft in the Supreme Court

Two years after the end of the Korean War in 1953, the draft law was put to an important vote of the Supreme Court in the case of *Witmer* v. *United States*. The case had begun on January 31, 1951, while the war was in full swing. On that day, Philip Andrew Witmer asked for conscientious objector status. He stated that he worked full-time in a hat factory and also that he worked on the family farm. He wanted a deferment from military service. In return, he promised to cultivate more acres of land for growing food. As a farmer, he claimed, he would contribute more to the war effort than he could as a soldier.

On his conscientious objector form, Witmer denied being a minister, stating instead:

My training and belief in relation to a Supreme Being involves duties superior to those arising from any human relation. This prevents me from turning aside from those superior duties which I owe to a Superior Being.[1]

To further support his claim, Witmer said he had studied the Bible. He had preached as a member of the Jehovah's Witnesses, a Christian sect that considers all of its members to be ministers. On February 21, 1951, however, his draft board rejected his claim. He appealed, and this time asked for a 4-D draft classification as a minister. The case was then sent by the appeal board to the Department of Justice and the FBI.

In its investigation, the FBI concluded that Witmer was sincere in his beliefs. At the Department of Justice hearing, a hearing officer reached the same conclusion. But the Department of Justice disagreed with this decision. The DOJ pointed out that Witmer had offered to contribute to the war effort through his work as a farmer. Therefore, his strict antiwar beliefs could not be sincere. The Department of Justice recommended a 1-A classification. This was upheld (agreed to) by the appeal board.

Philip Witmer still refused to appear for induction into the military. He was indicted for failing to submit to the draft. A federal court convicted him on this charge. A federal appeals court then upheld this decision. Witmer then appealed his case to the Supreme Court.

The case was argued before the Supreme Court on February 1, 1955, and decided on March 14, 1955. By a 7–2 vote, the Court agreed with the Department of Justice. In its opinion (written decision), the Court pointed out that Witmer had not claimed to be a minister on his original questionnaire. The Court also noted that the land Witmer had offered to plow for the war effort had lain fallow for twenty-three years. At his hearing, Witmer

*The U.S. Supreme Court decided a number of cases dealing with conscientious objectors. Shown are the justices who decided Muhammad Ali's case in 1971. (Thurgood Marshall, standing at left, did not take part.)*

had stated that "the boy who makes the snow balls is just as responsible as the boy who throws them."[2] If he really believed this, why had he offered to farm for the benefit of the war effort? His changing opinion about war convinced the Supreme Court justices that Philip Witmer's objection was not sincere, and his conviction as a draft dodger was affirmed.

## The Case of Daniel Seeger

Another important draft case reached the Supreme Court a few years after the *Witmer* decision. An important constitutional principal tested in this case was that of the Fourteenth Amendment to the U.S. Constitution, which requires "equal protection under the law." The courts interpret this to mean that all laws should apply equally to every citizen. It should not matter what a person's race, religion, or personal beliefs are. "Personal beliefs" include religious beliefs—or atheism. On these grounds, some have seen conscientious objector status, as defined in federal law, as unfair. They see it excluding those who did not belong to an organized church. It also seemed to exclude those who did not believe in any form of religion.

The Fourteenth and Fifth Amendments came into play in the case of *United States* v. *Seeger*. Raised in a devout Catholic household, Daniel Seeger had volunteered for service with the

American Friends Service Committee. This committee was a part of the Society of Friends, or Quakers. The Quakers had always held very strict views against war. Since the eighteenth century, lawmakers and the courts had recognized their church as a peace church. Seeger strongly approved of the Quakers' objection to war. But although he volunteered his services to the church, he never actually joined it.

In 1953, the Selective Service had classified Seeger as 1-A—fit for active duty. In 1955, this classification was changed to 2-S (student). In 1957, while still a student, Seeger registered as a conscientious objector. At this time, the conscientious objector questionnaire required the claimant to sign under this sentence:

> "I am, by reason of my religious training and belief, conscientiously opposed to participation in war in any form."

On his form, Seeger had struck out the words "training and" and put quotation marks around the word "religious":

> I am, by reason of my "religious" ~~training and~~ belief, conscientiously opposed to participation in war in any form.[3]

He followed this with another written statement. He claimed to be skeptical about the existence of God. But he also declared his "belief in and devotion to goodness and virtue for their own sakes, and a religious faith in a purely ethical creed."[4] Such a creed, in his view, did not demand belief in God.

Seeger's claim was denied because it did not include, according to the law, belief in a Supreme Being. To his draft board, he had violated the language of the law. The draft law at that time did not allow conscientious objector status for "essentially political, sociological, or philosophical views or a merely personal moral code."[5] In 1958, his draft board reclassified him as 1-A. He refused to report for induction and was tried and convicted for draft evasion. He then appealed his sentence. The federal appeals court reversed the conviction. The court held that the law violated the Fifth Amendment to the Constitution. In part, the Fifth Amendment states: "No person shall . . . be deprived of life, liberty, or property, without due process of law."

Violation of "due process," in this interpretation, meant Seeger had been unfairly tried, and found guilty, for his personal beliefs. He had a right, just as a church member did, to hold sincere and personal beliefs against war. To convict him, and not a religious believer, for such personal beliefs violated the Constitution, the appeals court said. The federal government disagreed. The government appealed Seeger's case to the Supreme Court.

The Supreme Court heard Seeger's case on

# Legal Terms

**amicus curiae**—Literally, "friend of the court"; someone who has strong interest in a case, but is not a party to it, may file an *amicus curiae* brief to present their point of view. Such briefs let the court benefit from the added viewpoint.

**appellate court** (also called court of appeals)—A court that reviews decisions of lower courts for fairness and accuracy. An appellate court can reverse a lower court's ruling.

**appellant or petitioner**—The person who feels the lower court made an error.

**appellee or respondent**—The person who won the case in the lower court.

**brief**—Written statement of a party's argument on one or more issues in the case.

**concur**—To agree with the majority in a court case.

**dissent**—To disagree with the majority in a court case.

**due process**—The constitutional doctrine that holds the state must give those accused of a crime a fair hearing and trial in the courts.

**equal protection**—The constitutional doctrine that holds the law and the courts must treat all citizens equally, whatever their race, religion, or creed.

**indictment**—The official charge of a crime by the government against the accused.

**majority opinion**—The ruling and reasoning supported by a majority of appellate court judges in a case. Concurring opinions are written by judges who agree with the majority opinion but have other reasons for their views. Dissenting opinions are written by judges who disagree with the ruling.

**opinion**—The written explanation of a court's decision.

**precedent**—A legal holding that will determine how courts decide future cases.

November 16 and 17, 1964. The decision in the case was announced on March 8, 1965. In their written opinion, the justices noted that Seeger was willing to refuse to appear for induction and go to jail. For this reason, his beliefs against war must be sincere. The Court also mentioned that Congress did not intend someone's definition of a Supreme Being to be the test of a sincere conscientious objector: "The objection to war is religious in nature, if it stems from objector's sincerely held moral and ethical beliefs held with the strength of orthodox religion."[6]

By this opinion, the Supreme Court found that sincere beliefs against war did not necessarily mean belief in God, or a Supreme Being. Seeger was sincere, the justices found. On his conscientious objector form, he had described his "religious faith in a purely ethical creed."[7] He backed up his claim by quoting philosophers such as Plato, Aristotle, and Spinoza. For these reasons, the Supreme Court affirmed the Court of Appeals decision finding Seeger a sincere conscientious objector. The final effect of the Seeger case was the rewriting of the federal draft law. In 1967, the mention of a Supreme Being was taken out of the law.

## The Case of Elliot Welsh

Another Supreme Court draft case covered ground very similar to the *Seeger* case. On June 1, 1966,

Elliot Welsh was sentenced to a three-year term in prison for evading the draft. The conviction was affirmed in an appeals court. Welsh then took the case to the Supreme Court. The case of *Welsh* v. *United States*, decided in 1970, tested the provision in the law that allows conscientious objectors by reason of "religious training and belief" but not by "political, sociological, or philosophical views or a merely personal code."[8]

Like Daniel Seeger, Welsh had altered his conscientious objector questionnaire. He had struck out the words "religious training" entirely. He claimed to have sincere beliefs of his own against participating in war. In the Supreme Court, he claimed that the conscientious objector statute violates the First Amendment clause of the U.S. Constitution, which begins: "Congress shall make no law respecting an establishment of religion. . . ."

Welsh claimed that the conscientious objector law, by requiring belief in a Supreme Being, made religious belief a test of his sincerity. He claimed to have no belief in God, a Supreme Being, or any other such notion of traditional religion. According to the First Amendment, in this view, his skepticism should not matter. Welsh backed up his claim by referring to the *Seeger* case. The Supreme Court agreed, saying that the draft could not exempt those who belonged to an organized church and deny such an exemption to those who did not. The exemption must be neutral and not favor one religion over another—nor could it favor believers over nonbelievers. Selective objection was still denied, but even atheists could now be conscientious objectors.

Supreme Court justices rely heavily on precedents (previous decisions). They use precedents to study problems and technicalities of the law. Past decisions guide them in making their present-day decisions. In general, a Supreme Court justice will not break precedent without very good reason. But at certain times, events create a condition of crisis in the courts and in the society at large. During the Vietnam War, the turbulent echoes of such a crisis rang through the somber halls of the Supreme Court. The widespread opposition to the war and violent racial strife in the cities had an impact on the justices who wrote their opinions.

In addition to *Witmer*, *Seeger*, and *Welsh*, three other Supreme Court cases created important precedents for *Clay* v. *United States*. In *Williams* v. *United States*, the Court decided that the Selective Service must use the individual's own interpretation of religious doctrine, not its own. The case of *Estep* v. *United States* involved objection to the Vietnam War, but not necessarily others. In *Estep*, the Court decided that a conscientious objector must oppose war in any form. Another case of the 1950s would become directly relevant to Muhammad Ali: *Sicurella* v. *United States*. Anthony Sicurella was a member of the Jehovah's Witnesses who asked for an exemption during the Korean War. Sicurella argued that the teachings of his church prohibited him from fighting for any earthly government. He would fight only in defense of the Jehovah's Witnesses and its members. In Anthony Sicurella's words, he would fight only "in defense of Kingdom interests."[9]

After hearing Sicurella's case, the Department of Justice had sent an advisory letter to the appeal board. It denied that Sicurella was a conscientious objector. But the advisory letter had not stated the grounds for this opinion. When the case reached the Supreme Court, the Court decided that the appeal board could not deny Sicurella his conscientious objector status. Sicurella may or may not have met the requirements of a true conscientious objector. But in the opinion of the Court, the vague advisory letter from the DOJ did not meet *its* requirements.

All of these cases laid the grounds for opinions on both sides in *Clay* v. *United States*. But the Sicurella case provided the justices with the most important legal precedent for a unanimous decision.

# chapter 5

# Fighting the Draft

The year 1955 was a time of peace, although tension between the United States and the Soviet Union still threatened war. With the coming of the 1960s, and a new conflict in a different part of Asia, the arguments over the draft and over conscientious objector status would grow angry and often violent. At the center of these arguments was a young boxer from Louisville, Kentucky, by the given name of Cassius Marcellus Clay.

## Getting Involved in Vietnam

By the elections of 1960, a young Massachusetts politician named John F. Kennedy attained the presidency of the United States. Young, handsome, energetic, and well-spoken, Kennedy represented optimism in a time of Cold War tension and doubt, a time when the United States saw itself locked in a vital struggle with the Soviet Union and the evil force of Communism. In his speeches, Kennedy promised a strong effort to combat the spread of Communism. He followed up these promises with actions. He visited the city of Berlin, Germany, divided by a wall of concrete and barbed wire between the Communist East and the U.S.-allied West. He ordered an invasion of the Communist-ruled island of Cuba, which failed disastrously. And he allied the United States with the government of South Vietnam.

Since 1954, when Vietnamese guerrillas (nonuniformed combatants) defeated a French occupation of their country, Vietnam had been divided between two governments, non-Communist South Vietnam and Communist North Vietnam. By the Geneva Peace Accord of 1954, the Vietnamese agreed to a division of their country between North and South. Although elections were to be held in 1956 to establish a unified national government, these elections did not take place. They were canceled out of fear of a Communist victory and the election of the Vietnamese Communist leader Ho Chi Minh as president. The North Vietnamese leaders still vowed to reunite the country and establish a Communist government by force.

In the 1950s, meanwhile, Cassius Clay was

developing into one of the best amateur boxers in the world. Born in Louisville, Kentucky, Clay had begun boxing at the age of twelve, on the advice of a Louisville police officer. In his teens, Clay won national championship bouts staged by the Golden Gloves and the Amateur Athletic Union. His success did not lessen the sting of segregation and racism he experienced on the streets of his hometown. In Louisville and many other southern towns, African Americans had to use separate schools and public facilities, such as buses, public parks, and swimming pools.

In 1959, while walking his hometown streets, Clay met a member of the Nation of Islam (NOI), who offered him a copy of *Muhammad Speaks*, the NOI newspaper. Clay bought the paper and the next day began reading it. The paper's columns and articles depicted American society as a system of racial injustice and oppression, an opinion that he agreed with. The Nation of Islam offered a way to resist and overcome this system by joining its ranks and following the teachings of a Chicago Muslim leader, the Honorable Elijah Muhammad.

Clay had been baptized in a Christian church, but he was not a practicing Christian. For his Christian acquaintances and family, religion seemed to hold little importance. Some attended church regularly on Sunday, while others did not. In Clay's eyes, very few Christians actually practiced their religion or obeyed its teachings in their daily lives. To him, there seemed no doubt that members of the Nation of Islam took their faith seriously. They did not smoke, drink, or use drugs; they dressed conservatively in dark suits; and they were taught to remain faithful to their families. The Black Muslims, as members of the Nation of Islam were known, strove for self-sufficiency, separate from the dominating economic system of the United States. They also preached the establishment of a nation within a nation, a society independent of the culture and customs of Christian, white America.

In the spring of 1960, Cassius Clay began training for the Summer Olympic Games, to be held that year in Rome, Italy. Because he

*The young Muhammad Ali was known as Cassius Marcellus Clay when he had his first amateur fight at age twelve.*

turned eighteen that year, he was required to take a written test administered by his local draft board. He did not take the test or the draft too seriously. At worst, he saw it as a distraction from the demands of training and sparring. The United States was at peace, and he knew that most of the top athletes got deferments or easy stateside assignments. At any rate, he failed the written test. As a result, he was classified as unfit for military service.

That summer at the Rome Olympics he won the gold medal in the light heavyweight division. He had gone as far as he could as an amateur boxer. When he returned home, he began a professional career. A syndicate of Louisville businessmen sponsored his training and his first professional bouts. That year, Clay also registered with the Selective Service System.

## Joining the Nation of Islam

Over the next three years, Cassius Clay won nineteen professional fights. But his most important encounter took place in Miami. In 1961, while he was training in that city, a member of the Nation of Islam named Samuel X. Saxon beckoned him into a NOI temple. There, a minister was delivering a powerful lecture on the evils of racism. Clay had not forgotten the Nation of Islam newspaper. He knew that many African Americans—including his brother Rudy—were joining and preaching this faith.

The lecture preached at the Muslim temple deeply impressed him. Clay attended more meetings of the Nation of Islam and visited the home of Elijah Muhammad in Chicago. Clay joined the Black Muslims, but friends, colleagues, and nearly everyone he knew opposed his decision. Many believed he was being used for publicity purposes by a corrupt organization that preached racial hate. Most whites, who were excluded from the group, believed the Black Muslims were organizing a violent revenge for America's history of slavery, lynchings, and racial oppression. They also viewed the Nation of Islam as disloyal, partly for its opposition to American involvement in Vietnam.

The United States was becoming more enmeshed in the Vietnam conflict. The government of South Vietnam, under President Ngo Dinh Diem, was resisting reforms in its economy and agriculture. The United States believed these reforms would strengthen the government in the south. Among its own people, Diem's government became more unpopular, as North Vietnam supported a strengthening guerrilla movement in the south.

President Kennedy was sending military advisors to South Vietnam to shore up that country's resistance to the Vietcong, the Communist guerrillas operating in the South. If

South Vietnam fell to the North and the Communists, it was feared, other Asian countries would go the same way. If the United States allowed an allied government to fall, it would lose influence and prestige to Communist China and the Soviet Union.

Humiliated by the failed invasion of Communist Cuba in 1961, Kennedy was determined not to allow another failure in Southeast Asia. He took seriously the vows he had made to spread democracy and resist totalitarianism around the world, and he saw Vietnam as a test of his own resolve. By the time of Kennedy's assassination in November 1963, the American military presence and influence in Vietnam was increasing rapidly.

In the meantime, with quick feet and devastating punches, Cassius Clay was fast becoming the most successful and famous boxer in the country. On February 25, 1964, he defeated Sonny Liston in Miami and won the title of world heavyweight champion. A week before this fight, he was called to take another draft exam at the Selective Service induction center in Coral Gables, Florida. He again failed the test.

## Draft Resistance

A flamboyant and expressive speaker, Cassius Clay enjoyed publicly taunting his opponents. With reporters and fans hanging on his words, he declaimed his own poetry to predict success in the boxing ring. He also grew more outspoken on the issues of race and segregation. To many African Americans, he was not only an athlete, but also a powerful representative of the entire African-American community.

But his outspokenness was widely resented, to say the least, by white sports fans and by the majority of middle-class Americans. They saw him as an upstart, and they did not like his brash, outspoken attitude. They especially did not like the new Muslim name he had taken after the Sonny Liston fight: Cassius X (later, the name would change again to Muhammad Ali). For many African Americans, family names—many of which originated with slave-owning families—represented a history of racism and discrimination by the white majority. Muhammad Ali saw "Cassius Clay" as a name he had discarded with his past, when he went along with his own family's conformity with white expectations.

From this time forward, Muhammad Ali tried to forget the name given him at birth. When he heard it, he ignored it. This rebellion—against his own family name and white society at large—reflected a much larger rebellion brewing against the Vietnam War. As the United States grew more involved in Vietnam, resistance to the war increased. Marches and demonstrations took place on college campuses. Crowds of protesters gathered in Washington, D.C., in front of government buildings and the Pentagon, the nation's military headquarters.

The protests did not dissuade President Lyndon Johnson, who took office after President Kennedy's death. Johnson vowed to save South Vietnam from Communism and, in 1965, sent the first U.S. ground combat units to the war. In 1966, a total of four hundred thousand men were drafted. In the following years, the number would rise dramatically. By 1968 more than half a million troops were in Vietnam.

Draftees were still a minority in the armed forces. But they made up nine out of ten infantry riflemen fighting on the ground in Vietnam. Deferments allowed college students, ministers, married men, and others to delay or avoid induction. The sons of wealthy and middle-class families could pay for college, or escape the draft altogether by fleeing to a foreign country, such as Canada or Sweden. As a result, most draftees fighting in Vietnam were members of the working class or minorities, who did not have as many options. To opponents of the war, the draft seemed to discriminate, on both ethnic and economic grounds. Even some war supporters saw the draft law as unfair, and deferments as unjustly favoring one class over another. The injustice of this system, and opposition to the war itself, stoked the fires of widespread draft resistance.

After 1965, resistance to the draft rose sharply. As casualty reports arrived with the evening news, students staged sit-ins, occupying classrooms and public spaces to show their opposition. Draft-eligible men opposed to the war burned their draft cards in public. Some took this resistance even further, breaking into the offices of local draft boards and burning their files.

In addition, more and more drafted men were claiming to be conscientious objectors. Judges, lawyers, draftees, and lawmakers still argued the proper meaning of "conscientious objector," as defined in the law. A few of these cases were reaching the halls of the Supreme Court. Most conscientious objectors did not argue their case as members of peace churches or on religious grounds. Most of them also refused any kind of noncombat service to replace military training and fighting. Instead, they refused to cooperate with the military in any way.

Some men deserted after joining the military and going through training. They objected to the war itself, although they did not mind military life or the prospect of defending their country, if necessary. One group of four deserters left their ship, the aircraft carrier U.S.S. *Intrepid*, in Tokyo harbor in 1967. Before fleeing to Sweden to escape the war, they assembled a press conference and announced the reason behind their actions:

> We oppose the escalation of the Vietnam war because in our opinion the murder and needless slaughter of civilians through the systematic bombing of an agricultural, poverty-stricken country by a technological society is criminal. We believe that the United States must discontinue all bombing and pull out of Vietnam, letting the Vietnamese people govern themselves.[1]

War supporters saw serving in the military and fighting in Vietnam as a patriotic duty. They saw

*Antiwar demonstrators protest at United Nations Plaza in 1967. Resistance to the war increased sharply after 1965.*

the defeat of Communism as vital to the national interest of the United States. To carry out this task, the military needed draftees as well as recruits for service. Draft boards were calling up men between the ages of nineteen and twenty-five, with the oldest called up first. But each had its own policy on how to select men for induction. To make the draft more fair, the Selective Service supported a national draft lottery, which would select men by a random ordering of their birth dates. President Richard Nixon proposed, and Congress passed, a lottery law in 1969.

Those who opposed the war strongly opposed the draft, however, whether it was imposed by a lottery or any other way. An individual's freedom of belief and opinion were paramount in America. If someone did not want to fight, he should not be forced to. During the war, about half a million men expressed this view by not cooperating with the Selective Service. About twenty-two thousand five hundred men were indicted for draft evasion. Of these, eight thousand were convicted and four thousand served jail time. About fifty thousand draftees fled the country, most to Canada. One draftee who would refuse to flee was Muhammad Ali. He would remain in the United States and fight his battle in the courts.

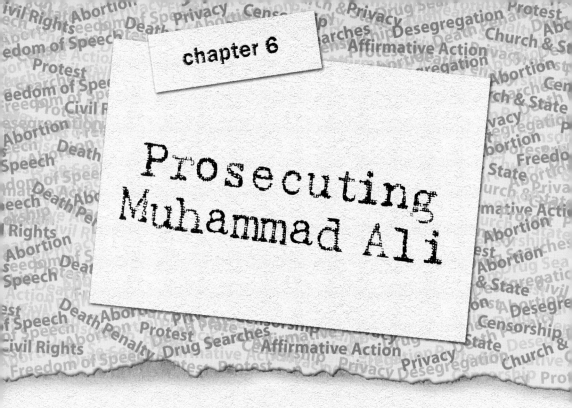

# chapter 6

# Prosecuting Muhammad Ali

In 1960, Cassius Clay had failed the written Armed Forces Qualifying Test and was classified as 1-Y, or deferred. In the early 1960s, he also had major hernia surgery. For these reasons, he did not spend much time worrying about the draft.

But as he attained and defended his world heavyweight title, the buildup in Vietnam continued. The draft issue was becoming front-page news. President Johnson was ordering more ground units to Vietnam. The military was pressuring local draft boards to increase the number of men classified as eligible for service. An increasing number of men were refusing to report for induction. Some were burning their draft cards. A few were going to jail.

In February 1966, Ali was living in North Miami and training for the third defense of his title as world heavyweight champion. His trainers were preparing him for Ernie Terrell, a heavyweight contender who would meet Ali in a Chicago arena. In the meantime, the Louisville draft board had lowered the passing grade on the Armed Forces Qualifying Test. The new passing mark fell just below the mark Ali had achieved six years before.

As a result, on February 17, the draft board reclassified Muhammad Ali as 1-A, fully eligible for the draft. He received a draft notice ordering him to report for induction. In a television press conference in Miami, he recited a poem to state his feelings on the draft and the war:

> Keep asking me, no matter how long
> On the war in Viet Nam, I sing this song
> I ain't got no quarrel with the Viet Cong.[1]

Ali's poem and opinion got headlines immediately all over the world. That same evening, callers rang his home phone in Miami continuously with threats and insults. Later, he also received calls of support. In his own words:

> in the days that followed, calls came in from Kansas City, Omaha, St. Louis, Las Vegas, New York, Philadelphia. Housewives and professionals and plain everyday people—who I never heard from except when I pulverized somebody in the ring—thanked me for what I said. Students called from campuses, urging me to come and speak. It

was a strange new feeling, and now, without planning or even wanting it, I was an important part of a movement I hardly knew existed.[2]

Ali's stance got him in deep trouble with the media. He was called a Benedict Arnold (an infamous traitor who turned over information to the British during the American Revolution). Other writers compared him unfavorably with Joe Louis, another black heavyweight champion, who had volunteered for the army during World War II. They questioned Ali's patriotism and worse, his sincerity. Gene Tunney, another former heavyweight champion, sent a telegram:

> YOU HAVE DISGRACED YOUR TITLE AND THE AMERICAN FLAG AND THE PRINCIPLES FOR WHICH IT STANDS. APOLOGIZE FOR YOUR UNPATRIOTIC REMARK OR YOU'LL BE BARRED FROM THE RING.[3]

Jimmy Cannon, a sports columnist, wrote:

> Clay is part of the Beatle movement. He fits in with the famous singers no one can hear and the punks riding motorcycles . . . the painters who copy the labels off soup cans and the surf bums who refuse to work and the whole pampered style-making cult of the bored young.[4]

For others, Muhammad Ali's actions were courageous. The champion was risking everything for his beliefs, and standing up to the world's most powerful government. The British philosopher

Bertrand Russell sent the boxer these prophetic words:

> In the coming months, there is no doubt that the men who rule Washington will try to damage you in every way open to them, but I am sure you know that you spoke for your people and for the oppressed everywhere in the courageous defiance of American power. . . . You have my wholehearted support.[5]

## A Struggle of Conscience

Much criticism of Muhammad Ali's opposition to the war had its origins in the public's view of his personality. For many, Ali was a little too brash and outspoken. As an athlete, he was generally expected to train relentlessly, perform to his physical limits, defeat his opponents, and otherwise keep his mouth shut. His poetry and his constant self-promotion irritated them, and his taunting and posturing in the boxing ring struck them as the marks of an egomaniac. As a member of the Nation of Islam, he had also become a representative of the black civil rights movement. His criticism of racism and of American institutions did not go down well with many public officials and journalists. Many people wondered why a man who lived by fighting could suddenly proclaim himself a man of peace—was his true, cowardly nature now appearing as he was faced with the possibility of fighting, and dying, for his country?

Ali's sheer self-confidence, and now his announcement against the war, touched off a landslide of anger and criticism. Many wanted him cut down to size, publicly and professionally. Ronald Reagan, the governor of California, tried to ban him from boxing in that state as an unpatriotic slacker. As a boxer, he was officially *persona non grata* (unwelcome) in California for several years.

Still, Muhammad Ali had options. During the draft crisis, one of his Louisville sponsors, Worth Bingham, invited Ali to a meeting. Bingham explained to Ali that the world heavyweight champion was a symbol, a representation of the entire country. The powers-that-be in the boxing world wanted their champion and symbol to be a model patriot and, if necessary, a soldier. Muhammad Ali wearing a military uniform would be good for boxing—a sport that had always suffered a serious image problem among the general public.

Bingham explained that Ali would never have to fire a shot in anger. Instead, he could enlist, go through basic military training, and accept a commission in the reserves. He could serve out his term of enlistment in the United States. He could keep himself in shape, put on boxing exhibitions, then return to the professional ring with a good reputation. He could obey the law and not risk a thing.

Over the following weeks and months, Ali gave

the idea a lot of thought. He knew that as a symbol of boxing, he would also become an example of the American justice system and of how it dealt with opponents of the draft. If he held to his stance, the military would turn him over to the federal government, which would undoubtedly arrest him, indict him, and probably find him guilty. It would surely be easier to simply go along with Bingham's suggestion and put in a year or two in uniform.

But as a member of the Nation of Islam, he was only supposed to serve in a holy war, a jihad, as declared by Muslims. Also, as a member, he was supposed to oppose the Vietnam War by any and all means. Personally, he did oppose the war; but professionally, he was determined to keep and defend his heavyweight title at all costs. His anti-war stance—as well as court fights, the loss of his boxing license, and jail time—might end his career for good. The call by his draft board had put Muhammad Ali into the longest and toughest fight of his life—a fight with his own conscience.

## Pressed to Apologize

The few lines of poetry he had recited to the press in Miami got Muhammad Ali into a world of trouble. In Illinois, Mayor Richard Daley of Chicago asked the governor to have the Illinois Athletic Commission review the license for the Terrell fight. The governor and the commission agreed but offered Ali a second chance. He was invited to make an appearance and explain himself to the boxing commissioners. Under pressure from pro- moters, sponsors, and trainers, Ali agreed. While flying to Chicago from Miami, however, he read newspaper articles explaining that he was ready to apologize for the remarks he had made in Miami.

The articles made him angry and even more determined to stick to his decision. When hauled up before the commission and pressed to apolo- gize, he refused. The Terrell fight, scheduled for March 29, was immediately banned in Chicago.

*Ali speaks with reporters at the Houston induction center. His stance against the draft angered many in the public and the media.*

Terrell then backed out of the fight, believing Ali would either go to jail, be banned from boxing, or both. To win the title, Terrell believed he may not have to actually fight for it. With state boxing commissions pulling his license around the United States, Ali next met George Chuvalo, the heavyweight champion of Canada, in Toronto.

In the meantime, Ali appealed his 1-A reclassification. In August 1966, he took his appeal to a circuit court in Kentucky. His lawyers argued that the induction was a violation of his constitutional rights, because African Americans were largely excluded from membership on draft boards. Ali also argued that he was a practicing minister of a recognized religious faith. The Kentucky court upheld the appeal, finding that Ali sincerely objected to the war on religious grounds.

The U.S. Department of Justice then put the Federal Bureau of Investigation on the case, ordering a full-scale investigation. FBI agents interviewed thirty-five people, including Ali's friends and business associates. The investigation was meant to determine if Ali was sincere in his application for CO status. The evidence gathered was then sent to the Department of Justice for a public hearing.

Judge Lawrence Grauman, a Kentucky circuit court judge, served as the hearing officer. Grauman heard testimony from Ali, from his mother and father, from a Nation of Islam minister, and from one of Ali's attorneys. He concluded that Ali was sincere in his objection on religious grounds and recommended that CO status be granted.

The Department of Justice did not accept Judge Grauman's recommendation. In an advisory letter, the government stated that Ali did not meet any of the three tests for CO status: whether it was based on religious beliefs, whether it was sincere, and whether Ali objected to all war, not just the one in Vietnam. He did not oppose war in any form, the letter stated, but only this particular war. According to the letter, Ali's beliefs

> do not appear to preclude military service in any form, but rather are limited to military service in the Armed Forces of the United States. . . . These constitute only objections to certain types of war in certain circumstances, rather than a general scruple against participation in war in any form.[6]

This was due to his "religious training and belief," according to the advisory letter:

> It seems clear that the teachings of the Nation of Islam preclude fighting . . . because of political and racial objections to policies of the United States as interpreted by Elijah Muhammad. . . . It is therefore our conclusion that registrant's claimed objections to participation in war . . . rest on grounds which primarily are political and racial.[7]

As for Ali's sincerity, the Department of Justice

expressed its doubts: ". . . the registrant has not consistently manifested his conscientious-objector claim. . . . his conscientious-objector claim was not asserted until military service became imminent."[8]

The Department of Justice sent its findings and Judge Grauman's opinion to the appeal board hearing Muhammad Ali's case. In March 1967, the appeal board voted unanimously to uphold the 1-A classification. In April, Muhammad Ali appeared at the Houston induction center. After refusing to step forward, he released a statement to the press:

> It is in light of my own personal convictions that I take my stand in rejecting the call to be inducted into the armed services. I do so with full realization of its implications and possible consequences. I have searched my conscience, and find I cannot be true to my belief in my religion by accepting such a call. . . . If justice prevails, if my constitutional rights are upheld, I will be forced to go neither to the Army nor jail. In the end, I am confident that justice will come my way, for the truth must eventually prevail.[9]

The World Boxing Authority stripped Ali of his heavyweight title and announced an elimination tournament to determine his successor. The New York State Athletic Commission also stripped him of his title, meaning he was no longer licensed to box in New York. Other state boxing authorities also took away his license. One by one, opportunities to defend his title disappeared. In May, a federal grand jury convened in Houston and indicted him on violation of the draft law. He was arrested, fingerprinted, and then released on five thousand dollars bail.

The federal trial of Muhammad Ali began on June 19, 1967. The government's prosecutor was Carl Walker, an assistant U.S. attorney. On the first day of the trial, the court selected six men and six women as jurors, with two men serving as alternates. None of the jurors or alternates was African American. On the second day, the government called its witnesses: three Houston induction officers and a Selective Service officer. The officer brought Ali's case file, which Judge Joe Ingraham allowed into the record as evidence. The defense then called two witnesses: two clerks from the Louisville draft board, who testified that the board was made up entirely of white members.

The trial took two days. In the late afternoon of June 20, the jury returned a guilty verdict after debating the decision for twenty minutes. Prosecutor Walker later remarked:

> The trial itself was cut-and-dried. Based on the law, the jury had to find him guilty. The only real issue was whether his 1-A classification had been proper, and that issue had been decided by the Selective Service system and reviewed by the judge. So the only question at trial was whether he'd permitted himself to be inducted, and of

course he hadn't. All the jury had to decide was whether or not he'd stepped forward to become a soldier.[10]

Before sentencing, Ali's lawyers mentioned that the boxer had only a minor traffic citation on his record. Otherwise, Muhammad Ali had a clean record with the law. Nevertheless, the judge imposed the maximum sentence of five years in prison and a fine of ten thousand dollars. Ali's lawyers immediately appealed his sentence, and the court allowed the boxer to remain out of prison on bail. Ali then pleaded to be allowed to go to Japan, where he had an offer of two hundred fifty thousand dollars to fight. His lawyers guaranteed that he would return immediately to the United States. The judge denied this request. He then confiscated Ali's passport, which prevented the boxer from leaving the country. He could not fight in the United States, and he could not fight in a foreign country. Even though he was still a free man, the government and the state boxing commissions, in effect, took away his right to earn a living at boxing—the only professional career he had ever known.

Ali did not stay out of trouble with the law, however. In December 1968, he spent ten days in Miami's Dade County Jail for driving without a valid driver's license—an infraction that for ordinary drivers carried only a fine. In the meantime, the boxing world needed more fights and more spectacles. The business thrived on controversy, and boxing promoters stepped in to take advantage. With Ali out of the profession, fight promoter Bob Arum organized a new boxing syndicate. Arum and his partners then arranged an elimination tournament to decide on the next heavyweight champion.

Ali's appeal of the sentence came before the New York District Court of Appeals on July 24, 1969. His appeal was denied. In the meantime, while still out of jail and on bail, he took part in three boxing matches. After the denial of his appeal in New York, Ali's lawyers filed for a *writ of certiorari*, or a plea for a hearing, in the United States Supreme Court. As grounds for a hearing, they claimed that his induction notice was based on an erroneous denial of his conscientious objector status. In the meantime, it was revealed that the FBI had been tapping Ali's phones and recording his conversations. To avoid hearing the case with this additional complication, the Supreme Court denied the writ of certiorari. The Court sent the case back down for another appeal and a decision on whether Ali's rights had been violated by the wiretaps.

In the meantime, Muhammad Ali became a cause for celebrities, authors, professional athletes, and anyone whose business it was to express an opinion. Author Irwin Shaw, in an article written for *Esquire* magazine in November 1969, entitled "Muhammad Ali and the Little People," stated:

> Until he won the championship from Sonny Liston, Clay was regarded as a handsome and not particularly dangerous clown. But after he won the championship in Miami and announced that he had taken the name of Cassius X (the Muhammad Ali came a year later) and that he was a Muslim, a member of the Islam religion, the . . . likable young underdog became overnight a dark threat to the nation's security and his continued deferral from military service an insult to the Flag. . . . to the ordinary American, especially the black American, it must seem that one man has been singled out. . . .[11]

The decision in the case of *Gillette* v. *United States* came down on March 8, 1971, while the Supreme Court was still considering *Clay* v. *United States*. As a conscientious objector, Gillette argued that he would be willing to fight for national defense. But he would not be willing to fight in Vietnam, which he saw as an unjust war. His conviction on draft evasion was upheld by an appeals court. On the same First Amendment grounds as *Welsh* v. *United States*, he took his case to the Supreme Court. Gillette argued that the draft law violated the constitutional ban on the establishment of religion.

According to the Military Selective Service Act,

passed in 1967, a conscientious objector must object to participation in *every* war, not simply those of his choosing. In its decision, the Supreme Court found this part of the law to be constitutional. Justice Thurgood Marshall wrote the opinion of the Court, denying Gillette's claim and stating:

> the impact of conscription on objectors to particular wars is far from unjustified. The conscription laws . . . are not designed to interfere with any religious ritual or practice, and do not work a penalty against any theological position. . . . And more broadly, of course, there is the Government's interest in procuring the manpower necessary for military purposes, pursuant to the constitutional grant of power to Congress to raise and support armies.[12]

The *Gillette* case was decided on the same day as *Negre* v. *Larsen*. In this case, the conscientious objector belonged to a church that favored "just" wars. The conscientious objector, however, refused to comply with his draft notice, stating that he personally opposed the war in Vietnam. The Court overruled his claim. The *Gillette* and *Negre* decisions dealt with the treatment of religion and individual conscience. As a member of the Nation of Islam, Muhammad Ali was also making a claim of conscience.

In the next month, the case of *Clay* v. *United States* came before the Court.

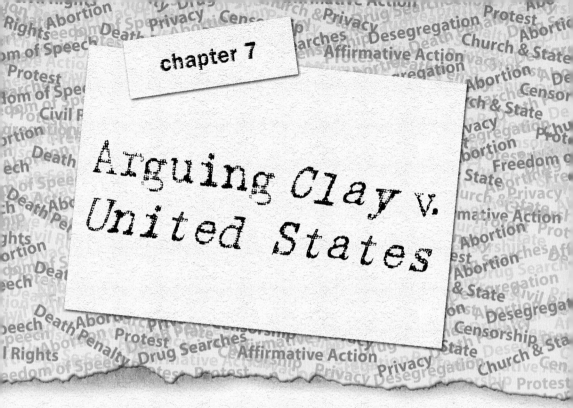

# chapter 7

# Arguing Clay v. United States

There was more to Muhammad Ali's draft case than the meaning of "conscientious objector." The Supreme Court heard the case while violent protests against the Vietnam War were occurring and the government was dealing with a rising tide of draft evasion. In every year since ground combat troops were committed, the number of draft evaders had increased. In addition, many American cities had experienced violent race riots. The case of Muhammad Ali focused these tough issues of race and an unpopular war. His sentencing by a federal court had not resolved the case.

Author Mike Marqusee describes the decision to hear Muhammad Ali's case in the highest court in the land:

Back in 1969, when the case first came before the Court, only one judge, Brennan, had been prepared to hear it, but the wiretap revelations had given the judges the excuse to defer the matter by sending it back to a lower court. Now, Brennan and others felt that there was no room for further evasion. Given the mood in the country, Ali had to be accorded a hearing in the Supreme Court before he could be jailed.[1]

At first, Ali believed himself at a disadvantage. The Court's Chief Justice, Warren Burger, had been appointed by President Nixon, whose actions as president and commander in chief of the armed forces Ali strongly opposed. (Nixon, for his part, looked on Ali as a draft dodger and wanted to make a harsh example of him.) Ali believed that Burger agreed with Nixon's stance and would try to see to it that Ali went to jail. In addition, the only African American on the court, Justice Thurgood Marshall, had recused (excused) himself from hearing the case. Marshall had been solicitor general in the Department of Justice when the government brought its case against Ali. This was a conflict of interest in the eyes of the law. A judge that has already dealt with one of the parties to a case, either legally or professionally, might feel personal bias one way or another. For this reason, a justice may recuse himself or herself from the case to avoid the appearance of an unfair decision.

Oral argument in the case of *Clay* v. *United*

*States* took place on April 19, 1970. Ali's lawyers argued for the petitioner. The solicitor general, Erwin Griswold, argued for the respondent—the United States. Griswold admitted that Ali may have been a sincere conscientious objector. He also admitted that Ali's objections to the Vietnam War were based on his religious training and belief. But he still argued that objection only to the war in Vietnam—and not to a jihad declared by Muslim leaders—meant that Ali was a selective conscientious objector.

*Ali addresses a gathering at a Nation of Islam convention in 1968. The U.S. government argued that while Ali's objections to the war were based on religious belief, they were selective, since he was not opposed to all war.*

Griswold argued persuasively before the Court. The justices met in their chambers four days later, on April 23, to reach a decision. On the first hearing, Ali lost his case by a vote of five to three. Justices William O. Douglas, William J. Brennan, and Potter Stewart had voted to support Ali's appeal; the other five justices voted to uphold conviction. Chief Justice Warren E. Burger assigned Justice John Marshall Harlan to write the majority opinion of the Court. But when Harlan set to work, things began to change.

Before writing his opinion, Harlan spent a few days reading the record of the Ali case. He also studied articles about the Nation of Islam and about the Muslim religion. One of the Supreme Court clerks had read *The Autobiography of Malcolm X*. Moved by the struggles of this African-American leader, the clerk asked Justice Harlan to read *Message to the Black Man in America*. The clerk explained that this book, written by Elijah Muhammad, would help the justice to better understand the Nation of Islam and its message. The book persuaded Harlan that the Department of Justice had misrepresented the beliefs of the Nation of Islam and of Muhammad Ali.

Justice Harlan came to see a parallel in *Clay* v. *United States* to the case of Anthony Sicurella, the Jehovah's Witness who had sought a draft exemption during the Korean War. Harlan wrote a memo to the other justices hearing the case and then changed his vote. This change of position caused a 4–4 tie, with Justices Harlan, Douglas, Brennan, and Stewart voting to reverse Ali's conviction. Chief Justice Burger and Justices Hugo Black, Harry Blackmun, and Byron White still voted to uphold.

The Supreme Court includes an odd number of justices to guarantee that no ties occur. In this case, however, Justice Marshall was not voting, and a tie had resulted. If the justices cannot resolve a case, then the petitioner—the party that brings the case—loses. A tie in *Clay* v. *United States* would mean that the conviction would be upheld, and Ali would go to jail.

Justice Potter Stewart argued that in *Clay* v. *United States* the Court had to reach a decision and resolve the case, one way or the other. To achieve this, Stewart seized on a change of position by the government. In front of the Supreme Court, Erwin Griswold had admitted that the first two grounds for denying Ali's CO status were invalid. The government now said that Ali was sincere in opposing the Vietnam War, and that this belief was based on religious training and belief. It still saw his objection to the war as selective, as he had stated his belief in jihad.

This represented a change of the government's position from the advisory letter, in which the DOJ had stated that Ali was insincere. In effect, the government was now saying the appeal board had been advised incorrectly. In addition, the appeal board had not stated its reasons for advising against Ali—legal grounds for overturning his conviction. With his eye on the nation's political and racial turmoil, Chief Justice Burger was persuaded to go along with this argument. By a unanimous 8–0 decision, Ali's appeal was upheld by the Supreme Court on June 28, 1971. The Department of Justice immediately dropped its charges and returned Ali's passport.

In the decision, the Court relied on the case of *Sicurella* v. *United States*. The opinion in Clay stated:

> Since the Appeal Board gave no reason for its denial of the petitioner's claim, there is absolutely no way of knowing upon which of the three grounds offered in the Department's letter it relied. Yet the Government now acknowledges that two of those grounds were not valid. And, the Government's concession aside, it is indisputably clear, for the reasons stated, that the Department was simply wrong as a matter of law in advising that the petitioner's beliefs were not religiously based and were not sincerely held.[2]

Justice Douglas wrote a concurring opinion. (A concurring opinion agrees with the decision of the Court.) In his opinion, Douglas quoted Muhammad Ali and his thoughts on jihad. Ali had testified that he was sincere and that he followed the teachings of the Koran against fighting on the side of unbelievers—even to the point of refusing to give a cup of water to a wounded non-Muslim.

Justice Douglas also wrote:

> The jihad is the Moslem's counterpart of the "just" war as it has been known in the West. . . . What Clay's testimony adds up to is that he believes only in war as sanctioned by the Koran, that is to say, a religious war against nonbelievers. All other wars are unjust. That is a matter of belief, of conscience, of religious principle.[3]

Muhammad Ali was now free to pick up his life and career where he had left it several years before at the induction center on San Jacinto Street in Houston. He went on to win several more spectacular matches, including the "Rumble in the Jungle" against George Foreman in 1974 and the "Thrilla in Manila" against Joe Frazier in 1975. Promoters staged these two fights outside the United States to help win an international audience to heavyweight boxing. But on February 15, 1978, in Las Vegas, an overweight and out-of-shape Ali lost his heavyweight crown to Leon Spinks. He won the title back in a rematch, and then retired in 1979. The many hard blows to his head during a twenty-year career in boxing damaged his nervous system and brought on a case of Parkinson's disease that still affects his speech and mobility.

Because the Supreme Court decision was based on a technical error in the Department of Justice decision against Ali, the case did not serve as a precedent for future decisions on the conscientious objector laws. Nor did the decision broaden the category of conscientious objector, in the eyes of the law. But on August 20, 1971, soon after the decision in *Clay* v. *United States*, the Department of Defense issued Directive 1300.6. It provided for granting CO status to anyone with "a firm, fixed and sincere objection to participation in war in any form or the bearing of arms, by reason of religious training and belief." The CO applicant had to meet three criteria. First and most important was a firm and fixed religious, ethical, or moral belief:

> Belief in an external power or being or deeply held moral or ethical belief, to which all else is subordinate or upon which all else is ultimately dependent, and which has the power or force to affect moral-well-being.[4]

This belief must object to war in totality: the conscientious objector must object to war in any form. He or she must also be sincere. The directive also expects such sincerity to be expressed by actions, speech, and writings in the past and present. Although not serving as a legal precedent, Muhammad Ali's successful case in the Supreme Court had convinced the military to revise its own guidelines on who is, and who is not, a conscientious objector.

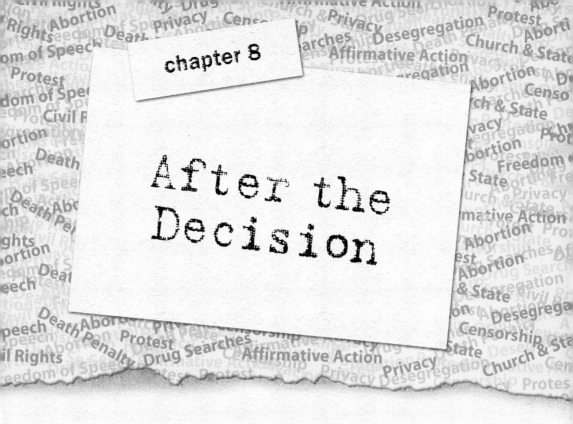

# chapter 8

# After the Decision

When he announced his objection to the Vietnam War and his refusal to join the army, Muhammad Ali found himself a controversial figure. Many boxing fans deserted him, seeing him as a coward and a slacker who had only dodged the draft out of self-interest. A common opinion was that Ali had used his religion as an excuse and had set himself above ordinary men who didn't have the money or fame to fight the federal government.

But as the war grew increasingly unpopular, Muhammad Ali's stand against it improved his image, not only in the United States but also around the world. Eventually, Muhammad Ali would be seen by a majority of people as a courageous individual who was willing to go to jail for his convictions. Leaders all over the globe invited him to visit. In early 1972 Ali flew to Libya to meet the Libyan president Moammar Qaddafi. Although Qaddafi was considered a despot and a trouble-maker by the U.S. government, Ali saw him as an important Islamic leader and a valuable ally of the Nation of Islam. During the visit, Qaddafi agreed to a $3 million interest-free loan to build a new Nation of Islam mosque in Chicago. In the mean-time, the reputation of the Nation of Islam was improving in Chicago. Mayor Richard Daley hon-ored Elijah Muhammad by naming March 29, 1972, Honorable Elijah Muhammad Day.

The stand of Ali and the Nation of Islam was helped by the fact that the Vietnam War was widely seen as a failure. The United States had not succeeded in driving Communist guerrillas from South Vietnam, nor had it prepared the South Vietnamese military to defend itself against the Communists. As the war dragged on, American politicians began looking for a good way for the United States to cut its losses and withdraw from the war.

On June 28, 1972, while campaigning for reelection as president, Richard Nixon announced that no more draftees would be sent to Vietnam. He ordered a withdrawal of the U.S. military, which continued until the last combat troops left Vietnam in August 1972. On August 28, Nixon announced that the draft would end in July 1973. The Selective Service canceled the lottery for the draft scheduled for 1973. In that year, the federal draft law expired and an all-volunteer force took its place.

Richard Nixon was reelected by a landslide in November 1972. The U.S. Congress then followed Nixon's lead on the draft. It provided for a standby draft in case of national emergency. Congress also passed a law requiring draft registration by young men turning eighteen years of age. The registration could be done by mail. In 1975, President Gerald Ford ended compulsory draft registration. In 1977, President Jimmy Carter signed a presidential pardon for all those convicted of draft violations during the Vietnam War.

In 1980, however, Carter found himself still fighting the Cold War. On June 27 of that year, the Soviet Union invaded Afghanistan. Soon afterward, at Carter's prompting, Congress reinstated compulsory draft registration. Supporters argued that registration would enable the military to act faster during a national emergency.

During the presidential campaign of 1980, Republican candidate Ronald Reagan had argued against compulsory registration. The Republican party called for a repeal of the registration law. Reagan argued that the military did not need draftees but better pay and benefits for its volunteers. After his election, however, Reagan changed his mind about draft registration. In 1982, he signed an extension of the law. In addition, the federal government began prosecuting men who failed to register. Most of those prosecuted and found guilty were sentenced to community service.

## Desert Storm and the Draft

After the Reagan administration, President George H. W. Bush ended prosecution for failing to register. But federal law imposed penalties for nonregistration. Those who refused to register could not apply for federal financial aid for students. By the Solomon Amendment, which took effect in July 1983, all men applying for federal financial aid for college must confirm they have registered for the draft. In some states, nonregistrants could not enroll in public colleges or universities.

In 1991, the United States again went to war. The Army and Marines invaded Iraq, a nation of the Middle East, after Iraq had invaded and conquered Kuwait, a U.S. ally. Bombing of Iraq continued during Desert Shield, while the following ground campaign—Operation Desert Storm—lasted just over a week. This operation proved a complete success. Yet the Iraqi leader, Saddam Hussein, remained in power.

There had always been a few hundred COs

among those who enlisted in the military. Although they had volunteered for service, they objected to the demands of their officers, or to being shipped to Saudi Arabia in preparation for an invasion of Iraq. During Desert Shield and Desert Storm, the number of CO applicants among those serving in the military increased. The first Army reservist to officially apply for CO status, Specialist Stephanie Atkinson, claimed she had joined the Army Reserve only for the education it offered and did not intend to fight. Atkinson was ordered to report to her unit, the 300th Adjutant General Company, and then prepare for shipment to Saudi Arabia. She failed to report, however, and was arrested. The Army turned down her CO application because of her refusal to report for duty but then released her, officially under "other than honorable" conditions. Other COs were reassigned to noncombat roles, allowed to remain in the United States, or simply discharged.

## Writing a New Draft Law

Lawmakers prepared for a new draft in the fall of 2001. This was just a few months after the terrorist attacks of September 11, 2001. The invasion of Afghanistan had taken place in October. This war was winding down, but the U.S. government was threatening Iraq with a second invasion.

The Universal Training and Service Act

required military service for all men between the ages of eighteen and twenty-two. The service would include basic training for up to a year. After that time, the draftees would be allowed to enter community service programs. COs would have to take part in basic training. They would not be required to undergo combat training.

The draft law had little support and did not pass. But in the spring of 2003, the United States again invaded Iraq. The attack succeeded, the Iraqi army was defeated, and this time Saddam Hussein was driven from power. The United States then occupied Iraq with its all-volunteer force: regular Army, Marines, and members of the National Guard. (The Guard trains its volunteers for part-time military service in the United States. Its units can also be called on to support regular military operations in foreign countries.)

The second Iraq war has not resolved as quickly as the first one. While Iraqis struggled to agree on a new constitution and resolve the country's many ethnic and religious conflicts, the U.S. military remained as an occupying force. The occupation was meant to guarantee a smooth transition from dictatorship to democracy. But forces within and outside of the country have opposed it. They have used rocket and mortar attacks, suicide car bombings, and assassination of Iraqis cooperating with the United States. These

*Muhammad Ali lights the Olympic flame at the 1996 Atlanta Olympic games. Though his stand against the draft had interrupted Ali's boxing career, it increased his fame worldwide.*

attacks have caused a high toll in American dead and wounded. In addition, a few American soldiers have claimed conscientious objector status. Although they volunteered for military duty, they now state their opposition to the Iraq war.

The occupation of Iraq has caused a sharp drop in volunteers for the military. In the first two months of 2005, the Army was short of 6 percent of volunteers it needed, the Army Reserve by 10 percent, and the National Guard by 25 percent.[1] The Army, Marines, and National Guard may remain in Iraq for several years, and the armed forces may need new members in order to carry out the occupation. As a result, some American leaders have considered returning to a military draft. Any new draft would draw on young men who still must register with the Selective Service when they reach age eighteen.

Politicians and military leaders hope that a draft will not be necessary. People forced to serve in the military do not make the best soldiers. In its own studies, the military has concluded that a draft would be a bad idea. The armed services need men and women trained in the use of computers and other means of "high-tech" warfare. Someone forced to serve, and reluctant to learn, would hinder a war effort instead of helping it.

In addition, a new draft for the Iraq war would be unpopular with civilians, who can vote politicians out of office. As it always has, the draft is causing a lively debate. On one side are those who see military service as a patriotic duty. Others see it as an unjust use of government authority. The case of *Clay* v. *United States* did not resolve this long-standing argument.

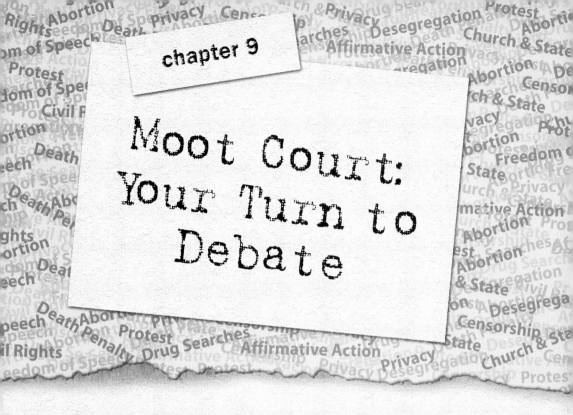

# chapter 9

# Moot Court: Your Turn to Debate

What is a "conscientious objector"? Do all men and women have a duty to fight for their country, if they are needed? Can they sincerely object to joining the military, and fighting? Should the government put conscientious objectors in jail? What is a fair and constitutional law on conscientious objectors?

A moot court gives you the chance to debate these questions. In a moot court, every student has an important role to play. Some will be lawyers, who will research the case and prepare "briefs," or written arguments. Some will be judges, who will hear both sides of the case and make a ruling. Some will be clerks, who help the judges prepare questions for the attorneys. Others act as reporters, who describe the actions in the court, interview those who take part, and write newspaper stories about the case.

This moot court activity deals with the law of conscientious objectors to the draft. This format can be used to argue and decide other important legal issues.[1]

# Step 1: Assign Roles

◇ Judges. If the group is large enough, have nine justices, as in the U.S. Supreme Court (even though the case of *Clay* v. *United States* was decided by eight justices). If there are not enough students, have a panel of three appellate (appeals court) judges. You may also invite a professional lawyer to take part as a guest judge. Choose one person to be chief justice and direct the proceeding. The judges will hear the attorney's arguments and pose questions they have prepared on the case. They will then write and deliver the final ruling. The majority opinion is the position agreed on by a majority of the judges' panel. Individual judges who agree write concurring opinions. Judges who disagree with the majority opinion write dissenting opinions.

◇ Court clerks. The clerks work with the judges to write five or more questions to ask the attorneys during oral arguments. Clerks also help the judges research their opinions. They look up past cases relevant to *Clay* v. *United States*. They find out how the two sides argued these cases and what rulings came down.

◇ Attorneys. Select two or more attorneys for the appellant, who argue that the lower court made a wrong decision. Also select two or more attorneys for the appellee, who feel that the lower court made a correct decision. One attorney from each side presents the argument (although any of the attorneys can answer questions from the judges).

◇ Reporters. They interview the attorneys before the case and write news stories about the facts of the case and the final ruling.

◇ The bailiff, who calls the court to order. The bailiff times each side's oral argument and prevents the attorneys from arguing past their allowed time.

# Step 2: Prepare Your Case

*Part 1: Gather Information*

The case you decide will be *Clay* v. *United States*. This Supreme Court case, heard in 1971, decided the fate of a famous professional boxer, Cassius Clay, who refused to join the United States Army during the Vietnam War. The Court had to decide if, according to the law, Clay (also known as Muhammad Ali) was a sincere conscientious objector to the war. The decision was unanimous, 8–0, in favor of Clay (Justice Thurgood Marshall recused himself from the case, as he had helped to prosecute Clay on the original charge of draft evasion).

The two sides—Clay and the federal government—did not dispute the facts of the case. Clay had been drafted by the Selective Service. He was ordered to report for induction into the military. But at a swearing-in ceremony in Houston, he had refused to take the draftee's traditional step forward. He was then charged with draft evasion, and convicted. The government stated that he was a "selective" conscientious objector, who objected only to wars of his own choosing.

According to laws dealing with conscientious objectors, a CO must be sincere in his beliefs; he must base these beliefs on religious training; and he must object to all wars, not just the one he is asked to fight. If a draftee asks for CO status and is refused, he can appeal. The appeal goes to the Department of Justice, which then conducts an investigation. The DOJ then advises an appeal board, which makes the final decision. During the Vietnam War, those found guilty of draft evasion faced penalties of up to five years in prison and a fine of ten thousand dollars. Although many young men fled to Canada and overseas to avoid the military or prison, Cassius Clay chose to stay home and fight his draft notice in the courts.

Everyone involved in the moot court activity should study the Supreme Court case *Clay* v.

*United States.* The case is published as 403 U.S. 698. That means that it is in volume 403 of *United States Reports*, the law reference that publishes all Supreme Court decisions. The case begins on page 698. The lower court case that was appealed in the Supreme Court was *United States* v. *Clay*, which can be found at 430 F.2nd 165. The federal law on the draft and conscientious objectors was at 62 Stat. 622, as amended, 50 U.S.C. App. 462(a). The law can be found in the 1964 edition of the United States code.

There are several important Supreme Court cases to study that dealt with conscientious objectors before and during the Vietnam War. These include *Gillette* v. *United States*, 401 U.S. 437; *United States* v. *Seeger*, 380 U.S. 163; *Welsh* v. *United States*, 398 U.S. 333; and *Witmer* v. *United States*, 348 U.S. 375. In these cases, conscientious objectors were tested on the sincerity of their anti-war beliefs and the basis of these beliefs in religious training.

*Clay* v. *United States* is important because a military draft raises tough questions on constitutional freedoms. If the U.S. Constitution guarantees citizens the freedom to practice their religion, how can the state force an individual to fight against his religious beliefs? To answer this question, the United States has been setting guidelines for conscientious objectors since colonial times. During the American Revolution, the members of certain peace churches were allowed to escape military service. Some had to provide alternate service, which kept them from fighting and possibly killing. During the Civil War, men with enough money could pay a substitute to fight in their place.

During the twentieth century, the law changed several times. Paying a substitute to fight for you became illegal. In addition, anyone with a sincerely held belief against war could legally claim to be a conscientious objector. The Supreme Court found the provision for members of peace churches unconstitutional, as it favored certain religious sects over others. By the time of *Clay* v. *United States*, membership in a recognized church was unnecessary to claim conscientious objector status.

Cassius Clay/Muhammad Ali's beliefs against war, however, were based on his Muslim faith. In the Islamic concept of jihad, or holy war, followers must fight only those battles decreed by religious edicts. The Vietnam War was not such a battle. Instead, the leaders of the Nation of Islam held it to be a racist and unjust war. Following this guidance, Muhammad Ali refused to participate.

*Part 2: Prepare Your Briefs*
A legal brief is a written presentation of your argument. Brainstorm with the lawyers on your team.

First, review the case. What are the facts of the case, and what were the decisions of the lower courts? What part of the Constitution is important to this case, and what exactly does it say? Which arguments can you use to make your case? How do the decisions in previous cases support you? What are the weaknesses of your case? How will the other side attack your own arguments? What are the possible consequences of a ruling in your favor, or a ruling that goes against you?

You may want to divide up arguments for research and writing. If so, be sure to work as a team to put the brief together. Otherwise, your brief may have holes or read poorly. Use these arguments as suggestions, and think of arguments of your own that might sway the opinion of the court in your favor.

In appealing his conviction, Ali claimed to be a sincere conscientious objector to war. That is, his objection was based on his true religious beliefs. He was not simply trying to avoid the military and the risk of harm or death on the battlefield. As evidence, he showed that he had been a member of the Nation of Islam since the early 1960s. As part of this conversion from Christianity, he had even changed his name—from Cassius Clay, his birth name, to Muhammad Ali, his Islamic name. His lawyers claimed that as a Muslim, he had the right—guaranteed by the Constitution—to hold to his beliefs and only fight in holy wars, as decreed by Islamic leaders. Further, they said, since the government never gave its specific reasons denying Ali his CO status, he was treated unjustly.

The government disagreed. The law on conscientious objectors was clear: One could not object only to the war one was asked to fight. One had to object to all war, any kind of military action, under any circumstances. For this reason, Muhammad Ali was violating the draft laws. Further, if the government needed citizens to fight, it should have the right to draft them. Every citizen should share equally in the burden of war—including young men who may be asked to risk their lives. The Department of Justice did not necessarily have to give its reasons for making a decision. Muhammad Ali was violating the law.

In real life, court rules spell out what briefs must contain. Use these rules for your moot court activity:

1. The cover page should have the case name *Clay* v. *United States*. Say whether it is for appellant (Cassius Clay, aka Muhammad Ali) or appellee (the government of the United States).

2. The text of the brief should have these sections:

   A. Statement of the issue for review: What question is before the Court?

B. Statement of the case: What is this case about? How did the trial court rule?

C. Statement of the facts: Briefly describe the facts relevant to the case.

D. Summary of the argument: Sum up your argument in 150 words or less.

E. Argument: Spell out the legal arguments that support your side. You can split this into sections with subheadings for each part. Include references to cases or authorities that help your side.

F. Conclusion: Ask the court to rule for your client.

3. Real appeals briefs may be thirty pages long. Limit your brief to no more than five typed pages, double-spaced, or about twelve hundred fifty words. If possible, type the brief on a computer. Otherwise, write very neatly.

4. On an agreed-upon date, each team gives the other side a copy of its brief. Each judge gets a copy too. If you do this in class, give the teacher a copy. Be sure each team member keeps a copy of the brief.

In real life, lawyers often prepare reply (or answer) briefs. These briefs answer points made by the other side. You do not need to prepare reply briefs. But you should study the briefs the other side has written and be ready to answer their points in oral argument before the judges.

*Part 3: Prepare for Oral Argument*

Participants should read carefully their own briefs and the briefs of the other side so that each point the briefs make is clearly understood. They should know beforehand how they are going to argue the case and get ready for any tough questions from the judges.

Judges should also read all the briefs before the oral argument. They should prepare questions for the lawyers. They should look for points in the briefs that are unclear or illogical. They should understand how each side is going to argue and how the sides intend to challenge their opponents. They should also understand the precedents in the case—the previous decisions that involve similar facts and arguments.

Each side will have up to fifteen minutes to argue its case. Practice your arguments together. Have one lawyer on your side play the part of your opponent. Have this person challenge your argument. Have one person play the part of a judge. Have the judge pose questions to both sides.

# Step 3: Hold the Oral Argument

*Part 1: Assemble the Participants*

◇ The justices sit together at the front of the

room. This is the bench. They should not enter until the bailiff calls the court to order. A speaking podium or lectern faces the bench.

⬦ The appellant's team of attorneys sits at one side, facing the justices.

⬦ The appellee's team of attorneys sits at the opposite side, also facing the justices.

⬦ The reporters sit at the back.

⬦ As the justices enter, the bailiff calls the court to order: "Oyez (oy-yay)! Oyez! Oyez! The _____ Court of the United States is now in session with the Honorable Chief Justice _____ presiding. All will stand and remain standing until the justices are seated and the Chief Justice has asked all present to be seated."

*Part 2: Present the Case*

⬦ The chief justice calls the case and asks whether the parties are ready. Each team's spokesperson answers, "Yes."

⬦ The appellant's spokesperson approaches the podium saying, "May it please the Court." Then argument begins. Justices interrupt when they wish to ask a question. The attorneys respectfully answer any questions asked. Do not get flustered if a judge interrupts with a question or an opposing lawyer makes a good point. Answer all questions honestly, and then move on.

⬦ Then the appellee's team takes its turn.

◇ Each team has up to fifteen minutes to present its argument. If the appellant's team wants, it can save five minutes of its time to rebut the appellee's argument. If so, the spokesperson should inform the court before closing its argument and sitting down.

◇ After the arguments, the bailiff tells everyone to rise as the justices leave to debate their decision.

◇ At this time, reporters may interview lawyers for the parties and begin working on their articles.

## Step 4: Publish and Report the Decision

After oral argument, the panel of judges decides who wins the case. A majority of judges must agree on the outcome. If students act as the judges, they should write an opinion explaining their decision. If a judge disagrees, that person can write a dissent. Any judge who agrees with the decision but has something to add may write a concurring opinion. The total length of all the opinions should be under five double-spaced typed pages. (Real judges' opinions are often much longer.) Copies of the opinions should go to the lawyers for both sides, plus the teacher.

If guest lawyers acted as judges, they do not have to write opinions. But ask them to tell your group what points persuaded them. They can also award certificates to teams for the best brief and for the best oral argument.

Reporters may interview the lawyers again, if they want to. Reporters' stories discussing the case and the outcome are due within twenty-four hours. Limit articles to five hundred words or less.

After the decision, the class should discuss the case and the arguments of each side. The class should discuss the Supreme Court decision and how it was made. They may also discuss the effects of the decision in society at large. In the case of *Clay* v. *United States*, the decision of the Court did not rely on a strict interpretation of the law. In addition, events outside the Court played a role. The bitter debates over the Vietnam War and racial strife taking place in American cities also influenced the judges.

# Questions for Discussion

1. The United States Constitution allows freedom of religious practice. But Congress has the right to declare war and to call up men to fight for the national defense. Should the law allow members of religious sects to avoid military service?

2. In the past, the law stated that conscientious objectors must base their stand on religious training and belief. Is it fair to exclude those who object to military service on a personal, nonreligious basis?

3. Islam's doctrine of jihad blesses those wars approved by Islamic leaders. Should the law allow a draftee, such as Muhammad Ali, to object to wars not approved by his religious teachers?

4. In the nineteenth century, draftees could hire a substitute to fight in their place or pay a "commutation fee" to the government. The fee helped the government pay for arms and for the wages of its soldiers. Was this practice just or wise?

5. At different times, the government has forced conscientious objectors to serve in a nonfighting role. They held noncombat jobs as medical

aides, transportation workers, clerks, and so on. Should a conscientious objector be forced to serve in the military at all?

6. During the first and second wars in Iraq, a few volunteer soldiers objected to fighting what they saw as an unjust war. Can a man or woman who volunteered for the military refuse to fight?

7. Does a military draft ensure that all citizens share the burden of fighting and defense of the country? Should anyone, such as married men or college students, be protected from the draft?

8. What kind of evidence should a conscientious objector show to prove that he is sincere?

9. Should the government punish those who refuse to register for the draft?

10. How does the military benefit from the draft, since draftees by definition are being forced to serve?

# Chronology

**1862**—During the Civil War, the U.S. Congress passes the Federal Militia Act, calling on the states to begin drafting men for service in militia companies. In the same year, the Confederate States of America also pass a draft law.

**1863**—Congress passes the Federal Conscription Act, setting down rules for commutation fees paid by those wishing to avoid military service.

**1864**—Congress passes the Draft Act.

**1917**—The draft returns after the United States enters World War I.

**1940**—Congress passes the Selective Training and Service Act, as World War II threatens U.S. involvement.

**1948**—Three years after the end of World War II, Congress passes the Selective Service Act, requiring men to register with their local draft boards.

**1953**—The Supreme Court case of *Witmer* v. *United States* decides against a conscientious objector for his lack of sincerity.

**1960**—Cassius Clay, an amateur boxer from Louisville, takes—and fails—a written qualifying test for the draft. That summer, he wins a gold medal in boxing's light heavyweight division at the Rome Summer Olympics.

**1961**—Cassius Clay encounters a member of the Nation of Islam, an organization founded by the Honorable Elijah Muhammad during the 1930s, and begins a conversion from Christianity to Islam.

**1964**—Clay fails another written qualifying test for the draft. One week later, he wins the world heavyweight boxing championship by defeating Sonny Liston in Miami. After this victory, Clay renames himself Cassius X, then Muhammad Ali, in recognition of his new identity as a member of the Nation of Islam.

**1965**—In *United States* v. *Seeger*, the Supreme Court finds that the law cannot deny conscientious objector status to those who do not belong to an established church. In the same year, the United States sends the first ground combat troops to Vietnam.

**1966**—On February 17, the Louisville draft board reclassifies Muhammad Ali as 1-A, fit for active duty. Ali is ordered to report for induction into the military. He appeals his draft notice, stating his objection on the grounds of membership in the Nation of Islam. The Department of Justice begins an investigation. At a Department of Justice hearing, a Kentucky circuit court judge finds Muhammad Ali to be a conscientious objector.

**1967**—The Department of Justice recommends that Ali's conscientious objector status be denied. In March, a Selective Service appeal board votes to uphold Ali's 1-A draft classification. On April 28, Muhammad Ali refuses to step forward at an induction ceremony in Houston, Texas. He is charged with draft evasion, convicted in federal court, and is released on bail pending an appeal.

**1969**—Muhammad Ali's appeal is denied in a New York District Court of Appeals. The court finds that he selectively objects only to the Vietnam War. His lawyers file for a hearing of the case in the Supreme Court.

**1971**—The case of *Clay* v. *United States* is heard in the Supreme Court on April 19. At the first vote of the eight justices participating, Clay/Ali loses the case. Before the Court's written opinion is made ready, however, several justices change their votes. On June 28, a unanimous 8–0 decision is announced in favor of Muhammad Ali.

**1972**—President Richard Nixon announces a withdrawal of the United States from Vietnam.

**1973**—The federal government ends the Vietnam-era draft. The military becomes an all-volunteer force.

**1980**—Jimmy Carter reinstates compulsory draft registration. By federal law, all men turning eighteen must register with the Selective Service. The law remains in effect.

# Chapter Notes

**Chapter 1. Defying the Draft**

1. Thomas Hauser, *Muhammad Ali: His Life and Times* (New York: Simon & Schuster, 1991), p. 169.
2. Ibid.
3. Ibid., p. 170.

**Chapter 2. War in Christianity and Islam**

1. George Sale translation, 9th ed., 1923, pp. 410–411.
2. John O'Sullivan and Alan M. Meckler, eds. *The Draft and Its Enemies: A Documentary History* (Urbana: University of Illinois Press, 1974), pp. 12–13.
3. Charles C. Moskos and John Whiteclay Chambers, II, eds., *The New Conscientious Objection: From Sacred to Secular Resistance* (New York: Oxford University Press, 1993), p. 30.

**Chapter 3. The Draft in the Twentieth Century**

1. Charles C. Moskos and John Whiteclay Chambers, II, eds., *The New Conscientious Objection: From Sacred to Secular Resistance* (New York: Oxford University Press, 1993), pp. 32–33.
2. Harlan F. Stone, "The Conscientious Objector," *Columbia University Quarterly*, vol. XXI, no. 4, October 1919, p. 269.
3. FindLaw, "*Bowles v. United States*," n.d., <http://caselaw.lp.findlaw.com/scripts/printer_friendly.p1?page=us/319/33.html> (September 22, 2005).
4. Heather T. Frazer and John O'Sullivan, "*We Have Just Begun to Not Fight*": *An Oral History of Conscientious Objectors in Civilian Public Service during World War II* (New York: Twayne Publishers, 1996), p. 40.
5. Moskos and Chambers, p. 39.

## Chapter 4. Testing the Draft in the Supreme Court

1. FindLaw, "*Witmer* v. *United States*," n.d., <http://laws.findlaw.com/us/348/375.html> (May 1, 2005).

2. Ibid.

3. FindLaw, "*United States* v. *Seeger*," n.d., <http://laws.findlaw.com/us/380/163.html> (February 20, 2005).

4. Ibid.

5. Ibid.

6. Ibid.

7. Ibid.

8. FindLaw, "*Welsh* v. *United States*," n.d., <http://caselaw.lp.findlaw.com/cgi-bin/getcase.pl?court=us&vol98&invol33> (July 31, 2005).

9. FindLaw, "*Sicurella* v. *United States*," <http://caselaw.lp.findlaw.com/scripts/getcase.pl?court=us&vol48&invol85> (July 31, 2005).

## Chapter 5. Fighting the Draft

1. Thomas Lee Hayes, *American Deserters in Sweden* (New York: Association Press, 1971), p. 17.

## Chapter 6. Prosecuting Muhammad Ali

1. Muhammad Ali with Richard Durham, *The Greatest: My Own Story* (New York: Random House, 1975), p. 124.

2. Ibid., p. 125.

3. Ibid., p. 143.

4. Robert Cassidy, *Muhammed Ali: The Greatest of All Time* (Lincolnwood, Ill.: Publications International, 1999), pp. 50–51.

5. David Remnick, *King of the World: Muhammad Ali and the Rise of an American Hero* (New York: Random House, 1998), pp. 287–288.

6. FindLaw, "*Clay* v. *United States*," n.d., <http://laws.findlaw.com/us/403/698.html> (May 1, 2005).

7. Ibid.

8. Ibid.

9. Thomas Hauser, *Muhammad Ali: His Life and Times* (New York: Simon & Schuster, 1991), p. 170.

10. Ibid., p. 180.

11. Irwin Shaw, "Muhammad Ali and the Little People," *Esquire*, November 1969, p. 102.

12. FindLaw, "*Gillette v. United States*," n.d., <http://laws.findlaw.com/us/401/437.html> (April 10, 2005).

## Chapter 7. Arguing *Clay v. United States*

1. Mike Marqusee, *Redemption Song: Muhammad Ali and the Spirit of the Sixties* (New York: Verso, 1999), p. 261.

2. FindLaw, "*Clay v. United States*," n.d., <http://laws.findlaw.com/us/403/698.html> (March 15, 2005).

3. Ibid.

4. Department of Defense Directive Number 1300.6, from Defense Technical Information Center, August 20, 1971, <http://www.dtic.mil/whs/directives/corres/pdf/d13006wch4_082071/d13006p.pdf> (May 12, 2005).

## Chapter 8. After the Decision

1. Edward Epstein, "Support Grows for Beefing up U.S. Forces," *San Francisco Chronicle*, April 4, 2005, p. A-1.

## Chapter 9. Moot Court: Your Turn to Debate

1. Adapted from Millie Aulbur, "Constitutional Issues and Teenagers," *The Missouri Bar*, n.d., <http://www.mobar.org/teach/clesson.htm> (December 10, 2004); Street Law, Inc. and The Supreme Court Historical Society, "Moot Court Activity," 2002, <http://www. landmarkcases. org> (December 10, 2004); with suggestions from Ron Fridell and Kathiann M. Kowalski.

# Glossary

**commutation fee**—During the Civil War, the money paid by men to the government to avoid the draft.

**conscientious objector (CO)**—A person who avoids military service by sincere beliefs against war.

**conscription**—The selection of citizens to join the military by the government.

**deferment**—Temporarily avoiding the draft by falling into certain draft classifications.

**draft evasion**—Illegally avoiding induction into the military.

**exemption**—Avoiding the draft entirely by falling into certain draft classifications.

**induction**—The process of joining the military via the draft.

**jihad**—The Islamic doctrine of holy war, which can be fought in defense of the faith or to convert nonbelievers.

**just war**—The Christian doctrine that holds that believers may take part in certain wars, such as those fought in self-defense and those that have as their goal a just and lasting peace.

# Further Reading

## Books

Ali, Muhammad, with Richard Durham. *The Greatest: My Own Story*. New York: Random House, 1975.

Galt, Margot Fortunato. *Stop This War! American Protest of the Conflict in Vietnam*. Minneapolis: Lerner Publications, 2000.

Meltzer, Milton. *Ain't Gonna Study War No More: The Story of America's Peace Seekers*. New York: Random House, 2002.

Meyers, Walter Dean. *The Greatest: Muhammad Ali*. New York: Scholastic Press, 2001.

Stout, Glen. *Muhammad Ali*. New York: Little, Brown, 2005.

## Internet Addresses

### African-American Involvement in the Vietnam War: Muhammad Ali

<http://www.aavw.org/protest/ali_alivus_abstract08.html>

### Muhammad Ali: The Greatest of All Time

<http://www.ali.com>

# Index